ETHICS FOR TEACHERS AND MIDDLE LEADERS

Every school has a mission statement based on values and ethical beliefs. *Ethics for Teachers and Middle Leaders* sets out a way of thinking through the key issues of ethics in teaching and shows how a school's ethical values can be translated by students and staff into action. It is designed to help rehearse certain ethical dilemmas and guide teacher leaders in helping others to think through and develop appropriate behaviours.

Chapters consider the role of ethics in all aspects of school life including teacher professionalism, teaching methods, lesson planning and assessment. This book not only examines everyday concerns such as class management and presenting curriculum ethically, but also touches upon emerging issues in e-learning, career building, leadership and school governance.

Packed full of real examples from schools and opportunities to reflect, the book will help readers to understand how their behaviour, decisions and advice to others might be guided and to avoid some of the common pitfalls in school. This insightful book will instil confidence in teachers and middle leaders as they face such ethical dilemmas in their daily work.

Trevor Kerry has been a teacher in primary, secondary and further education. He worked for several innovative government-funded projects, as well as being a teacher educator, LEA senior adviser, and academic. He has written more than thirty education texts and is Visiting Professor in Education at Bishop Grosseteste University, Lincoln.

'This is a highly readable and engaging book that explores the ethical issues and dilemmas that teachers and school leaders face on a daily basis at school. In straightforward language and a crisp and flowing style this profoundly insightful book explores a series of contemporary issues that will provide a useful resource in any teacher education course and/or school-based professional development workshop.'

Dr Christopher Bezzina,
University of Malta and Uppsala University, Sweden

'This text is a welcome addition to the literature on ethics, specifically for those in leadership or aspiring to leadership in the school context. Written in an engaging style by an author with extensive experience of both research and practice, the book brings together up-to-the-minute insights from that experience and roots them in the work in schools. It is essential reading for everyone involved in teaching and learning in the ever-changing complex world of education. The reader is guided to reflect on their own practice and by so doing is led on a journey of ethical discovery.'

Peter Neil, *Vice-Chancellor,*
Bishop Grosseteste University, Lincoln, UK

ETHICS FOR TEACHERS AND MIDDLE LEADERS

A PRACTICAL GUIDE

Trevor Kerry

LONDON AND NEW YORK

First published 2021
by Routledge
2 Park Square, Milton Park, Abingdon, Oxon OX14 4RN

and by Routledge
52 Vanderbilt Avenue, New York, NY 10017

Routledge is an imprint of the Taylor & Francis Group, an informa business

© 2021 Trevor Kerry

The right of Trevor Kerry to be identified as author of this work has been asserted by him in accordance with sections 77 and 78 of the Copyright, Designs and Patents Act 1988.

All rights reserved. No part of this book may be reprinted or reproduced or utilised in any form or by any electronic, mechanical, or other means, now known or hereafter invented, including photocopying and recording, or in any information storage or retrieval system, without permission in writing from the publishers.

Trademark notice: Product or corporate names may be trademarks or registered trademarks, and are used only for identification and explanation without intent to infringe.

British Library Cataloguing-in-Publication Data
A catalogue record for this book is available from the British Library

Library of Congress Cataloging-in-Publication Data
Names: Kerry, Trevor, author.
Title: Ethics for teachers and middle leaders : a practical guide / Trevor Kerry.
Identifiers: LCCN 2020048361 | ISBN 9780367682477 (hardback) | ISBN 9780367682484 (paperback) | ISBN 9781003136606 (ebook)
Subjects: LCSH: Teachers–Professional ethics. | School administrators–Professional ethics. | Teaching–Moral and ethical aspects. | School management and organization–Moral and ethical aspects.
Classification: LCC LB1779 .K47 2021 | DDC 371.1–dc23
LC record available at https://lccn.loc.gov/2020048361

ISBN: 978-0-367-68247-7 (hbk)
ISBN: 978-0-367-68248-4 (pbk)
ISBN: 978-1-003-13660-6 (ebk)

Typeset in Bembo
by KnowledgeWorks Global Ltd.

CONTENTS

	List of tables	vi
	About this book	vii
	Foreword	x
1	Ethics: In schools, in life, in education	1
2	Ethical professionalism in social context	14
3	The ethical school's approach to class management	24
4	Ethical curriculum	42
5	Ethical pedagogy	64
6	Ethical lesson planning, assessment and homework	83
7	Ethics and e-learning	98
8	Ethical career patterns	111
9	Ethical middle leadership	121
10	Ethical governance	133
11	The only way is ethics	145
	Finis	153
	Notes and references	155
	Index	160

TABLES

5.1 Components of an effective explanation 82
6.1 Planning a lesson with an eye to ethical outcomes 95
10.1 Audit document: Aspects of an ethical school 140

ABOUT THIS BOOK

This is a book about ethics in education. It is aimed at both teachers and middle leaders in schools; but also at an important additional readership – teachers in training. Trainees will spend little (or no) time on this subject yet will quickly find themselves in situations demanding ethical awareness the moment they move into schools (for those accessing school-led teacher education, this will be immediately). From time to time the book will mention the Senior Leadership Team and whole school issues: this is inevitable since the school is the context within which teachers and middle leaders operate. The text deals mainly with primary and secondary schools.

The idea for the book had its genesis in another volume which I was writing, about middle leaders in schools. It occurred to me that ethics play a large part in the life of teachers and teacher leaders but nearly all the texts on this topic, however worthy, are relatively academic. I wanted to put together something which would appeal to practitioners because it combined sound knowledge and research on the one hand, but accessible style and some opportunities to interact with the text on the other. In this, sometimes turgid, field I wanted to communicate that it was fine to smile occasionally, and that the topic had daily relevance. It is a contentious area: it's inevitable that you will not agree with everything that is said – feel free to debate with yourself and others, to peel away anything you see as author bias.

In adopting a suitable style for the book, I have opted to try to keep a light touch by blending sound theory and advice with relevant insights from literature. Quotations come from education texts; but some allusions emanate from more general literature where the authors make analytical comments which are relevant to the ethical themes dealt with here. (Copyright Law prevents direct quotation of this general literature, but you can easily follow up anything that interests you via Google).

Examples of school-based situations that prove ethically challenging are used throughout. Anecdotes told to me by individuals are used with permission but not attributed. Other examples of ethical dilemmas are based on real events but are anonymised; changes are often made to location, teaching phase, gender of participants and so on, on a random basis. Often the text has a narrative form, occasionally in the first person, or addressed directly to the reader: it is a volume that comes out of experience, practical examples (albeit anonymised), and useful metaphors.

There needs to be a health warning: and it is an important one. Ethics may sound like a purely theoretical topic, and one which is distanced and bland. It is not. Ethical decisions are about real, and sometimes painful, dilemmas in the three-dimensional world, which will condition our choices and actions. It is a warts-and-all subject; it demands that a reader is prepared to face dilemmas honestly: it pre-supposes discussion, debate, disagreement, speaking truthfully, coming to hard conclusions, and admitting that not all the answers are clear nor can they be prescriptive. To use a modern (and rather unpleasant, but apt) phrase: it is no place for snow-flakes; nor for those with closed minds, prejudices, or opinions that will not bear rigorous deconstruction. But all that should excite, rather than put off, a reader. After all, we have just outlined important facets of intellectual integrity. We all want our students to develop that, so we must, too.

The text is broken up into quite short episodes denoted by sub-headings. The intention is for the reader to dip in and out of the book, not necessarily to read it sequentially or in one sitting. Notes and references are kept to an absolute minimum, indicated by [] and a number, and listed at the end of the text. It is a book to put in your pocket for a gruelling trip on public transport or to keep by the bed for episodes of insomnia. It is, in short, a kind of *vade mecum*. The intention is also to provoke some thoughts which the reader will find inspirational or at least encouraging.

The text requires you to interact with it. In each chapter you will find one or more sections labelled ACTION. At this point you are asked to carry out a theoretical (i.e. thinking) or practical task about the topic under discussion. Whether you do so or not is your choice; but you may get more from the book if you do. Leaders might find the ACTION sections might also serve as sets of issues to discuss with colleagues as a way of standardising ethical actions across a department or faculty.

It is worth repeating: since this is a book about ethical dilemmas the material will be both controversial and open to interpretation. There are often no wrong or right answers, though some courses of action may be better than others. Decisions are often nuanced, not definitive. Debate is the essence of true education – treat the material in that way. If the scenario presented looks biased to you, that may be deliberate, and may be part of the ploy to keep you exercising critical judgement. The book will avoid the tabloid newspaper approach to ethics: the sweeping headline and sensational twenty-four-hour issue. It works even harder to bypass the pejorative slanging-matches that characterise most of social media.

The intention of the book is to help you acquire structures for thinking through ethical problems; it does not provide 'answers' because every ethical situation is contextually different.

Various colleagues showed faith in the project. Annamarie Kino at Routledge signalled an immediate interest. Colleagues, too, were supportive: Fr Mark Ellul, head of the Archbishop's Seminary in Rabat, Malta, former colleague Professor Angela Thody, and John Richardson, a Lincolnshire head teacher. Dr Carolle Kerry, as always, generously entertained my obsession with writing and provided insights from her considerable experience as a former primary school governor and Chair of Governors. My thanks to them.

If you gain from this book you can tell me how @LancasterDV403.

FOREWORD

A huge amount of human effort, revenue and materiel are expended on education. It is, therefore, imperative that a good job is made of it. Yet the voices of sceptics such as John William Gardner (1912–2002), who was Secretary of Health, Education, and Welfare under President Lyndon Johnson, will not be silenced. His image of education was of giving students bunches of flowers when we should be teaching them grow plants. In the UK, the call is for testable 'facts' rather than independent learning, thinking and understanding. Those whom we charge and trust with our education services must have vision, rather than becoming bogged down in the measurable and the orderly. Nor should we be led astray by social media websites, where notions of what is 'right' or 'good' degenerate into slanging matches advocating ill-considered opinions. This book is about ethics in education: about the ethical behaviour of teachers, the ethical approach of Society to education, and the ethical standards our young people acquire through their education. If we value Society we cannot afford to fail our students (quite literally, the future depends on it); and no aspect of our educational endeavours is more controversial or more quintessential than those encompassed in the debates about ethics. Yet it is an area in which training is minimal and practice is confused, challenging and changing. To grasp these issues is critical for our intended audiences: trainee teachers, qualified teachers and middle leaders who form the front line of the system.

ETHICS
In schools, in life, in education

INTRODUCTION: ETHICS AND HOW THEY APPLY TO EVERYDAY LIFE

This is a book about ethics as they impinge on our work as educators. Ethics affect us in our daily lives, and in our professional lives. To set the scene, let's begin somewhere else:

I will choose the location and you can choose the venue. The location is a four-star hotel. You can put it anywhere your fantasy takes you. It's breakfast time.

Freda and Fred (like all the other couples in this little narrative) have signed up to the half-board tariff; they have come down to breakfast, and then will while away the day (on the sun loungers, at the nature reserve, on the beach, in the amusement arcade, surfing, camel riding – you choose) until they return ready for pre-dinner cocktails. (Don't know about you – I'm liking this place already.)

Breakfast is a veritable feast, the choices of hot food are augmented by a groaning buffet.

Freda and Fred enjoy a hearty breakfast; something they don't have time to linger over at home. Over the second pot of coffee Freda disappears to the buffet and returns with a sweet, pink apple and a chunky banana: she secretes them (having first surreptitiously looked around the breakfast room) in her capacious handbag under the table. She says to Fred: 'If you were to go and get a slice of that nice Madeira cake and a Danish pastry we wouldn't have to buy any lunch'. He does. They don't.

At the next table are Joyce and Dick. They observe, unobtrusively, the actions of Freda and Fred and disapprove. They enjoy the breakfast, and after the hot course make sure they eat plentifully of the buffet. She enjoys two pears; he manages three croissants. It is way beyond anything they would eat at home, but it will keep them going until dinner is served tonight.

Further along the row of two-seat tables sit Arthur and Arthena. They eat their normal cereal choices, then enjoy a hot course, and he tops it off with an indulgent slice of toast.

Later, in the local town, all three couples encounter, at various times, two engaging students from the local university sociology department who are conducting a survey. Each couple answers independently all the questions on the survey. One question is: Have you ever stolen anything? They all answer 'No'.

> **Action**
>
> Consider the extent to which you agree with their individual answers.

I hope you enjoyed that brief vacation at the beginning of this book, but it is time for work now.

The story above raises the everyday questions of ethical behaviour.

Freda and Fred, as deduced from their behaviour, thought they were doing something wrong, but they still did it. They might have felt that they were breaking some externally imposed norm about not stealing (because the food was not for their breakfast, but they used it as a way of saving money later); the hotel may even have had a published policy about taking food from the breakfast room as opposed to eating in the breakfast room (some hotels do, to circumvent just such an eventuality as has been described). They both answered 'No' to the sociologists. Since they both seemed to have felt that they were flouting a norm, they were both dishonest in this. Fred may have felt that he was less culpable than Freda 'because it was her idea' and he was just a passenger (his middle name was, coincidentally, Adam). In both cases, the food was not theirs to take – for the purpose for which they took it. Secretly Fred justified the action of his partner with the thought that 'the hotel cost an arm and a leg, so all's fair in love and war'. At the end of the interview, he chatted to the pretty girl about this and that while he was waiting for Freda, and said he was interested they were doing a survey on theft because only last week, back home, he had had his Rolls taken off the drive and he felt bastards like that ought to be locked up somewhere where the key would go missing. They all parted on very good terms. The girl sociologist said to the boy sociologist: 'Nice couple. It's wrong when honest people like that get their goods removed by criminals'.

Joyce and Dick enjoyed their encounter with the sociologists, too, secure in the knowledge that their consciences were clear.

For Arthur and Arthena – well, for Arthur anyway – the encounter was a bit less happy. When it got to the question about stealing he had to admit, to his shame, that as a kid he had been in trouble for scrumping – so he couldn't answer 'No'. What he didn't say was that he was the child of a one-parent family with minimal income who spent much of the time not just hungry but half-starved.

Now, you have had an everyday introduction to the problems of ethics in daily life.

CLARIFYING SOME SIMPLE TERMINOLOGY

We ought to clear up here and now some issues in terminology. The key words are: ethics, morals, norms, values.

There is a distinction between ethics and morals; but it is hard to discern the difference in much that is written or spoken on the subject. In this book I am going to make a valid (but personal) distinction and try, for consistency's sake, to stick to it.

- **Ethics** – refer to the carefully thought-out, well-articulated, theoretical principles or philosophies on which a person's behaviour is based. It is not that behaviour, it is the rationale or philosophy on which that behaviour is built.
- **Morals** – refer to the individual's standards of behaviour which he/she chooses or attempts to adopt as a result of the beliefs he/she holds about the principles that should govern behaviour (ethics). Morals are personal, individual standards or aspirations that operationalise ethical beliefs. (If you wanted to be cynical you might say that ethics are the high ideals of personal behaviour, while morals are frequently failed attempts to achieve them.)

- **Values** – it seems to me, are the habitual morals by which one lives and judges others. I will use the term in this limited sense and attempt to avoid the ambiguities which are often associated with the word. Above all, I will not use 'values' and 'ethics' interchangeably: they are not the same thing. That might mean I use the word ethics rather a lot – but better repetition than lack of clarity.
- **Norms** – are slightly fuzzy at the edges conceptually, but are the generally accepted standards and behaviours adopted by a society or Society (I use the word society to denote the people among whom we habitually live, work and socialise; Society for the more amorphous and impersonal concept of the wider group within which we claim identity, e.g. a Nation). They will probably overlap with the categories above but may not be identical with them. For example, an individual may accept all the usual precepts of the Society not to kill, steal, lie and so on; but acting on different compulsions (maybe those of their religion) they may feel it reasonable to discriminate against certain classes of people – recently publicised cases of shop owners refusing on religious grounds to supply goods to gay people epitomises this conflict.

The distinction made above between ethics and morals, if sustained, will iron out quite a lot of ambiguity in the discussion about ethics generally and, later, about ethics in education specifically.

So where do ethics, and thus morals, come from? Most favoured candidates are religion, society and/or some group, sect or similar body which adopts specific ways of behaving based on identified belief systems. We'll take a glance at all these options:

Religion: Most religions claim to have a knowledge of the divine which includes injunctions on how humans should behave – this would be true of Buddhism, Islam, the Bahai faith and so on, and in the United Kingdom, traditionally, Christianity. The religious doctrines provide the theoretical underpinning (ethics), from which emanate the codes of behaviour (Ten Commandments in the Jewish faith, for example), which in turn form the morality the religion tries to adopt. To complicate matters, there is a substantial overlap between religions on ethical issues but no consensus; and even within religions, sectarianism often splits opinion on even quite key ethical issues (cf. the attitude of Protestants and Catholics towards birth control, outlined later in the chapter).

Society: Religions may influence a Society's ethical and moral stances; and many behaviours are enshrined, subsequently, in the law of that particular nation or ethnic group. So religion and law interplay with Society's role in forming an ethical position, i.e. about what is right and wrong. But there are pragmatic considerations, too. Generally (but not universally), not killing people on a routine basis is seen as a pragmatic solution to a more secure Society. This might become a 'norm' – i.e. behaviour we would expect of fellow citizens. Secular codes of ethics or 'moral' behaviour often look suspiciously like the religious ones, but that's because, at root, they are all striving towards the same or a similar goal.

Groups, cults, sects: Any widespread and influential collection of people might, over time, influence the way society thinks about problems we class as ethical issues. Socrates tried to analyse 'the good' and attempted to envisage Utopia. There is a growing Humanist movement in the UK, and this eschews religious values – yet its ethical stance is not a million miles different from Christian religious principles on the majority of issues.

To reject wholly any ethical position at all and its resulting moral behaviour – whatever that is – is tantamount to anarchy; and anarchy is usually destructive of Society and gets its wings clipped. But we have seen that to say that ethics are 'broadly similar' across many religions and cultures does not rule out some very major differences of view, differences of motivation, or disputes about detail and sometimes even about fundamentals. Hence, ethics are not as clear-cut in practice as they might appear in theory. Things can be ethical but not legal; legal but not ethical; ethical but not in tune with specific religious morals; in tune with religious morals but not ethical; ethical but not in step with the norms of Society, and so on. In ethics (at least in their practice), there are no black-and-white images of life, only shades of grey.

Action

Think about an ethical conflict you may have experienced in your own life, maybe within your own family. Such conflicts can be very distressing. How was the conflict resolved? Was it, indeed, resolved? If so, what was the path to successful resolution? If not, why not? What barriers could not be overcome?

ETHICAL DILEMMAS ILLUSTRATED

The conflicts relating to an apparently 'simple' ethical issue can be demonstrated even in relation to the most fundamental principle of ethics, the prohibition about killing:

- First, we make a distinction between killing in cold blood and killing with a (justifiable) cause – i.e. between murder and killing in extenuating circumstances
- That distinction is further blurred by the notion of manslaughter (unintentional killing)
- Even murder attracts the views that there are 'degrees' of culpability, e.g. killing while the balance of the mind is disturbed; killing with and without motive or intent
- Then there is 'legal' killing – e.g. in war

Individuals are often presented with scenarios:

- Would you kill someone if they were seriously threatening your life (self-defence)?
- If they were threatening someone else's life?
- If failing to defend your country might mean enslavement of you, your loved ones and your fellow citizens?
- Then again, there are the issues around euthanasia …

I could go on – but you get the point.

It is not hard to appreciate that, in life, what seems at first glance a simple prohibition is surrounded by the fog of uncertainty and the miasma of complicated debate: not least, because ethics in practice (morals) involve motivation – and that's a highly contentious area.

SOME APPROACHES TO SOLVING ETHICAL PROBLEMS

The rest of this text is primarily concerned with ethics in education contexts: with those things which impinge on teacher professionalism, teachers planning curriculum and teaching it, and with teacher ethical behaviour against the background of classroom, school and career. Ethical debate is a concern for all teachers, and for those who manage and lead teachers in carrying out those activities. We have seen that it is a complicated and multifaceted affair. The book is not about how to teach ethics to students, but much of what is said will impinge on the notion that teachers are role models for students in the ethical sphere as in others; so the issue will be re-visited briefly in Chapter 11. Before we end this chapter, we shall look at some generic examples of ethical dilemmas in education settings, and you will have the opportunity to practise some skills in analysing the situations painted in the scenarios. First, though, it will be useful to sum up the argument so far. What have we learned to date about gaining ethical insights into problems and issues, especially those in the sphere of education?

Begin with an open mind: First, it is better to begin with an open mind that is with questions, not answers: what, when (i.e. in what context), who, how, why, to what ends, with what intentions?

Ethical decisions are often messy and compromises: Second, we have identified that, while in some cases, an ethical decision may be clear-cut, usually it can be couched only in what are really shades of grey. While, when we look at the 'big questions' of right and wrong, goodness and evil, love and hate, killing and not killing, answers may appear relatively easy and obvious, in reality the smaller ethical dilemmas are more 'messy' and less tractable. In the cold light of everyday, it is not possible always to attain the absolute Good and we may have to accept the best that can be achieved.

The key skill lies in deconstruction: Leading from this insight, my third proposition is that a critical skill is that of de-construction: we need to learn how to pull a situation apart to understand it fundamentally. The questions we ask – as well as those above – must include questions about what we know of the situation as well as what we don't know; often these questions will take us into the realms of motivation of those involved, too (even our own in making judgements about the situation).

Avoid predetermined schemes: The fourth proposition leads from the three already cited; the most productive starting point in reviewing any ethical dilemma consists of asking questions to deconstruct the issue. That, in turn, means it does not start from a pre-determined set of 'moral' beliefs. These personal beliefs (which we all have and usually live by) are likely to emanate from either a religion or a philosophy. In solving ethical dilemmas in daily life and educational settings there are rarely ready-made answers. Our personal beliefs may form a context for later reflection on the dilemma, but they are not the route to its solution.

[I know that some readers may find this last paragraph a touch disturbing. For this reason, I will try to exemplify what I mean. I was brought up in the Christian tradition in what remains an officially Christian country: Christianity predicates its beliefs on a holy book; in these things Christianity replicates many other religions. The New Testament element of Christianity's holy book lays down principles about sexual behaviour (actually, some of the statements are self-contradictory – but that is a different debate, albeit a very significant problem). However, Christianity has traditionally been split over a key notion of sexual behaviour – birth control; different wings of the Church take diametrically different views on the matter. Nor is it possible to sidestep the issue by saying that there is another Christian principle of not killing which covers the dilemma – that is a kind of special pleading, and the logic peters out on closer scrutiny. Christian denominations and even Christian countries are divided about this issue. Clearly, a book written in the 1st century cannot give us specific answers to individual issues two thousand years later. So, any fair-minded person would have to conclude that the New Testament proves a broad framework of ethical principles, but leaves us to work out the detail in our personal decisions. Nor is Christianity alone. A colleague and I had an interesting conversation with a Jain, who was explaining the ethical principles of his religion – the most significant of which is non-violence. The Jains try to kill nothing, even sweeping beetles aside so that they do not kill them. Then he announced he was driving to London next day. My colleague asked him: 'Aren't you going to kill a lot of insects on the journey, for example, by smashing them on your windscreen?' He replied that, regrettably, he was; but in the real world there are always compromises to be made. So, the point I want to make about beginning from a religious/philosophical given is: by doing this we have not begun with an open mind, we have already muddied the waters.]

A FIRST LOOK AT SOME ETHICAL SCANARIOS

You will have discovered for yourself, at this stage, that there are two major aspects to an ethical dilemma: the 'theoretical answer of the ultimate good' on the one hand, and the need to take practical decisions and actions on the other. A quick glance at the literature of ethics in education will discover that much of it is either immensely learned but relatively turgid, or else not immediately tailored to teachers' everyday needs. The intention of this book is to avoid both pitfalls. For this reason, having discussed some of the theory, the remainder of this opening chapter will take scenarios based on real events and interrogate them for insights into the workings of ethics in the everyday life of schools.

> ### Action
>
> Three scenarios follow, each of which presents an ethical dilemma for you to consider. Imagine you are the manager who must decide what action to take about the events described. In each case read the Scenario first; and consider how you might de-construct it and move towards a view or a solution. Once you have formulated some thoughts, read the Commentary and review your thinking. Finally, read the section What else you might want to know. At this point you should have a good grasp of the issues and at least a few clues about how to resolve the dilemma.

> ### Scenario 1: Social media revenge
>
> *Incident:* A series of posts on a social media website began to appear just before the summer vacation period. These posts began as low-level innuendo about 'a scummy teacher' at an anonymised school: Alanadale. Neither the posts nor the information in them were very specific, but they gradually gained a following. As the new school year approached the scope of the posts widened and more staff were implicated, and then names (it was not clear to the general reader whether these were true or false names) were added. Just after the start of the new term a specific nickname was used for the key victim in this series of posts, and then a barely covert description of some events which had happened in this nicknamed teacher's life beyond the school gates. The posts had now attracted quite an audience; and it became clear that someone was pillorying a real teacher in a real school. Rumours began to circulate in the school about who was using a false identity to cover up their

campaign of vilification. The perpetrator was eventually unmasked. It transpired that the member of staff who first featured in these posts was about to get married at the time they started. In a conversation with one of the students she had made a cutting remark about that student's marital prospects: there had been a history of bad blood between the two of them because the teacher had previously accused the student of being scruffy and dirty.

Commentary: Teachers are open to more threat than ever before if they upset students: threats do not have to be physical. From the evidence presented, much of this incident arose out of a slight, real or perceived, from the teacher. It is impossible for us to judge whether the slight was real (i.e. a deliberately cutting remark), whether it was unintended (just clumsiness on the teacher's part), or the result of over sensitivity on the part of the student (a bit of joking gone wrong). The degree of culpability attaching to the teacher really depends on knowing about the original incident. The student's response is calculated. The fact that it starts relatively mildly, with somewhat distanced innuendos, but then escalates, suggests a determined attempt to settle the score. We cannot judge from the information provided whether any of the student's remarks or allegations are true; nor is that the prominent issue. However valid the student's grievance, though, this was not the way to deal with it. There are potentially legal implications such as libel underlying this.

What else you might want to know in judging the actions here: Certainly, the full circumstances and intention of the teacher's remark which triggered the student's reaction. Probably, more information about the student, and whether there was any history of similar behaviour. Also, whether this student had complained previously about any staff member and had the complaint dismissed out of hand.

Scenario 2: Principal enjoys the high life

Incident: In an academy for secondary students, the school gained a formidable reputation for high-level academic results; and the students were exemplary in their turnout and demeanour. The female principal took on expansionist plans; she used the reputation of the school to take over other, less well-performing, schools. Soon this thriving conglomerate was running on a budget of huge proportions. The principal decided that it was time to provide even more expansive opportunities for the students than were currently available, and purchased with academy money a large property on the Trough of Bowland so that rotas of students could visit there for residential work in geography and as an inspiration for creative arts. Of course, the centre needed a residential caretaker, and an appointment was made who later emerged to be a close relative of the principal.

Commentary: Again, the ethical situations depicted run into questions of law, and of professionalism. The principal's initial actions seem to be both well-planned educationally, and educationally successful. Employing a relative always leaves open the issue of 'conflict of interests'. On the face of it, this situation is ethically questionable but, subject to certain conditions, could be legally acceptable.

What else you might want to know in judging the actions here: There are a lot of unanswered questions here. We would need to know the detail of the advertising processes for the appointment, how the job criteria for the appointment were established (i.e. was the job 'tailored to a pre-determined candidate?'), how the interviewing panel was constructed, whether the relationship of principal to applicant was known to the panel. One might also enquire as to whether the salary offered was appropriate to the post, or inflated beyond what might be expected. There are also questions of motivation – e.g. was the whole residential centre idea a long-term ploy by the principal to provide for a struggling relative? Though a scenario like this would not be for staff to judge in any formal sense, the action of the principal might fairly be construed as casting doubts on the integrity of other staff members (by way of putative association with a 'corrupt' organisation), and may affect the way in which students were perceived by outside agencies: the consequences of the actions of an individual may not be confined to that individual.

Scenario 3: Cheat in the exams

Incident: Every member of staff wants their students to do their absolute best in public examinations; most will do everything possible to ensure that able youngsters have the best possible start in life. Only a minority, however, turn a blind eye to students cheating. But it does happen; in one case a teacher suspected that a student had managed to use technology to bring critical information into the examination room. Though the teacher, Mr X, was aware of the student's use of the device during the exam, he turned a blind eye. However, a fellow invigilator blew the whistle on the matter when the exam finished, and Mr X was subject to a disciplinary proceeding. At the hearing he said he had done it for two reasons: he believed the student, who came from a particularly unsupportive home, had massive potential which would eventually free him from his negative environment; further, he had personal experience of unsupportive parents – he wanted to help the student overcome his problems with which he felt a close empathy.

Commentary: Cheating by a teacher to promote their own results, those of their groups, or of individuals are all contrary to professional norms (more of these later). What seems to operate in this case is a (mis-placed) sense of duty: the teacher (rightly) wants to do his best for the student (he doesn't seem to have much to gain for himself), but allows various levels of empathy to cloud his judgement. One has to reckon, too, with the fact that, when a situation like this comes to light, some colleagues might be sympathetic to the teacher because they might despise a government-sponsored testing system, so the whistleblower might fare worse with colleagues than the perpetrator. His comments about his own background show the teacher has not managed to hold his emotional response at arm's length.

What else you might want to know in judging the actions here: As a leader, I would want to know whether this incident was unique in the relationship between this student and the teacher; and maybe, whether it was the tip of an iceberg – i.e. were other staff and other students working similar scams? There's also the issue of cheating on behalf of one student can be construed as disadvantaging other students either directly or indirectly. I would also want to explore the parameters of this teacher-student relationship which led to such an extreme breach of conduct.

SUMMARY

This opening chapter has tried to do three things: to define the nature of ethics and clarify our terminology; to exemplify the ethical problems that occur in all our lives and to begin to apply ethical thinking to the education context. In the process we have seen that the norms of Society, the law and professionalism standards, plus any religious or philosophical beliefs we may hold, impinge on solutions to ethical problems – and it is important to be aware of the roles these factors play. In the next chapter we explore the relationship between professionalism and ethical behaviour in more detail.

2

ETHICAL PROFESSIONALISM IN SOCIAL CONTEXT

ETHICS AND CODES OF CONDUCT

The outside world might reasonably expect that a member of the teaching profession could be in trouble for infringing a professional code if he/she had sexual relations with a student, swore at a class for misbehaving, or threw a missile at a student who was not paying attention. The same members of the public, and indeed teachers themselves, might be a bit more taken aback if they discovered that a teacher was breaching a professional code by answering a student's question about Donald Trump's competence, by not enquiring about the health of a colleague's elderly relative, or by failing to eat a piece of offered cake. Yet all of these scenarios are possible and have been the subject of complaints.

Professions, like teaching, medicine, dentistry, practising law and so on, are generally governed by a Code of Conduct; the respective Codes will set out principles on which interactions between the professional and the client should be based. There are a number of different Codes relating to teachers across the developed world, but all will contain substantial similarities. Codes of Conduct encapsulate expected teacher behaviour; and so they enshrine the required ethical behaviour of teachers. The Codes are not of themselves a set of ethical principles – they do, however, represent the kind of expected behaviours of teachers which emanate from the ethical norms prevalent in the Society in question. These Codes cover more than teaching, learning and curriculum because, as a fundamentally interpersonal relationship, teaching is subject to a range of activities each of which makes behavioural demands on the professional. Unsurprisingly then, in England, the teachers' Code of Conduct is divided into two sections, each subdivided as listed:

TEACHING – A teacher must:

- Set high expectations which inspire, motivate and challenge pupils
- Promote good progress and outcomes by pupils
- Demonstrate good subject and curriculum knowledge
- Plan and teach well-structured lessons
- Adapt teaching to respond to strengths and need of pupils
- Make accurate and productive use of assessment
- Manage behaviour effectively to ensure a good and safe learning environment
- Fulfil wider professional responsibilities

PERSONAL AND PROFESSIONAL CONDUCT – A teacher should:

- Uphold public trust in the profession
- Have proper and professional regard for the ethos and policies of the school
- Understand and act within statutory frameworks

While other Codes in other places may express things differently, the messages are much the same. The small print of the Codes spells out what is meant by the broad categories. In the first chapter, we discovered that ethics were the standards expected of citizens in Society; these Codes of Conduct spell out for teachers the standards which are expected within their professional contexts. They are, though, subject to alteration and change, just as the expectations of Society change; they are not set in stone, but rather a movable feast subject to interpretation. This characteristic makes them hard to tie down to a simple set of totally transparent rules. You can look up the current Code of Conduct for teachers in England (https://www.gov.uk/government/documents/teachers-standards); to spell out the detail would be rather boring but the gist appears in what follows. Our concern here is rather about how this and similar Codes might be interpreted in practice.

CENTRALITY OF STUDENTS TO CODES OF EDUCATIONAL CONDUCT

Fundamental in most instances is the ethical principle that students stand at the heart of the teacher's concerns and activities. Broken down into its component parts, this might demand that teachers become role models, with qualities such as responsibility, loyalty, honesty, integrity, respect and concern for equality high on the list of elements which guide and mould students' conduct. But teacher detachment follows from this: acting towards students impartially, accepting diversity, being free from partiality or prejudice and performing their roles in a trustworthy manner. This last might include a degree of confidentiality; though this can be tempered if the situation requires the intervention of a principal, education specialist or the law.

Of course, student progress will be high on the teacher's ethical agenda – the progress of all students encouraged to be fulfilled to the best of their ability. So will issues like student health and safety, their mental well-being, the safety and security of the learning environment, freedom from bullying of any kind and respect for all. Teachers will need to have a mind, too, to appropriate teaching and learning methods, assessment and recording – all of which support students' progress.

A typical Code will make professional demands: it will require teachers to carry out contracted duties, to further professional competence by participating in in-service training, to support school events, to be loyal and supportive to the school and colleagues, and act in these matters with integrity – even, perhaps, to be conversant with statutory requirements. It may encourage participation in wider learning opportunities for the teacher himself/herself that will enhance their competence or career progression. There may be a general requirement in support of the reputation of the profession in the eyes of the public, but especially of students, parents and other professionals.

In addition, if teachers join a Professional Union or a Learned Society relating to teaching, they may be required to agree to other requirements by that organisation. (You can easily google any organisations you belong to and find out what their regulations say.) Increasingly, there is a realisation that the ethical use of technology is incumbent on teachers.

All of this may seem detailed enough, but things are not always what they seem on the surface. In Society at large, we have the rule of Law; but even the Law is subject to interpretation by judges on a case-by-case basis: Statute on the one hand and case law on the other. It is at this stage that things get complicated. For this reason, the next segment of the chapter looks at some publicised principles in real scenarios (in all cases in this text, people, locations and events have been anonymised and do not purport to give accurate details of specific incidents for legal reasons).

ETHICAL RELATIONS WITH STUDENTS

Action

Read the three cases below. Your job is to consider in each Case (a) whether you would have regarded the behaviour suitable for a teacher, middle manager or head as appropriate; and (b) to contemplate the extent to which you agree with the outcome as reported. In each Case, probe the range of ethical issues which apply; use them in your judgement about the Case. Each Case reflects reality but has been anonymised and altered in order to protect individuals.

Case 1 Befriending students appropriately on social media

There have been quite a number of cases where teachers have used social media to contact students outside school. The situation is complicated because schools have very varied policies on this: some prohibit any e-contact with students outside school; others allow such contacts; while some simply stay quiet about the issue. The contact usually takes the form of either communication via social media sites, or the passing of email messages. In this particular case, a male member of the teaching profession was discovered to have had a running correspondence with a female student using email outside school hours. A quantity of messages was found when a parent became suspicious. The messages did not contain any impropriety and the teacher was given a formal warning.

Case 2 Alleged sexual relations

A female teacher was arrested on suspicion of sexual relations with several students. The students had been on a school trip and were on the return journey by ferry. Miss Y was described as a twenty-three-year-old teacher of languages in her second year of teaching. She had volunteered to assist with the school trip. During the overnight crossing, she had allegedly been intimate with three teenage boys under the age of consent. When the party got home, one of the boys became concerned and told his parent. Miss Y was banned from the profession; she was given a one-year jail sentence.

Case 3 Let them eat cake

A primary school head was having a difficult time winning over staff members in a new job. Over time the staff collected a number of complaints about the head, alleging that he was unsuitable to run the school. The issue went to Governors. Among the accusations were that after a member of staff had been absent because of a family illness and then returned to work, the head had failed to ask after the sick husband. This was cited as evidence of his uncaring attitude. Relationships were sometimes strained with other individual staff members: on one occasion the staff sent him in a cup of coffee at breaktime, together with a slice of cake from a function attended by the staff member. The head did not eat the cake and it was returned with the empty cup. The staff member thought this insulting. The Governors called a disciplinary meeting to discuss staff complaints and eventually, the head was dismissed from his post.

Cases like these are just a few among many which are heard by the Teaching Regulation Agency each year. If you Google this organisation you can read all of the procedural documents which they produce; they explain how schools can proceed against teachers who default on the Professional Code. Some cases are serious enough to go to Law. The site does not give details of individual cases, but they are often reported in the Press. What may surprise you is the apparent inconsistency of many of the judgements against teachers. (Hopefully, by reading this book, you will avoid such problems; but if you are accused of any misconduct, your first port of call is your Union.)

BEING ETHICALLY PREPARED

It is a mistake to assume that, in your career, the worst will never happen. The chances are it won't, but that will be because you are aware of the need to subscribe to the Code of Conduct and because you have some idea about the intricacies of obeying not just the broad principles of it, but some of the minutiae too. You will have acquired what has been called 'ethical literacy' – and it will serve you in good stead. These ethical pitfalls are like quicksand; and, like quicksand, you can slide into the trap easily but getting out may be difficult. A colleague of mine saw this beginning to happen to a student-teacher when they were supervising:

> I went to the school several times to see Mr J. He was a mature man (older than me), an excellent teacher and a really nice guy, who had been made redundant from another profession. But he was not versed in the ways of young people. On one visit, I noticed a female student hanging around after the lesson: I had to wait for her to talk to him at length before I could comment on his teaching. A week or so later, at the end of a lesson with the same class of fifteen-year-olds, she again way-laid Mr J. She was a touch more circumspect this time because I was present; but she leaned over the desk rather too close to Mr J and asked if she could arrange a meeting with him later so that he could correct some of her work, as she didn't understand his comment on it. Mr J agreed on a time. When the student had left, I said to Mr J: 'You do realise you are being chatted up by this student, don't you?' He was completely taken aback, and a little embarrassed. From that point on he took action to ensure that all their contacts were in public.

The Professional Code of ethics for teachers is designed substantially to protect the rights of the students. It is important for trainee and young teachers to understand professional ethics and values before entering the teaching profession. But the Code is also important as a shield for the teacher – and inexperienced teachers ignore it at their peril.

★

Why is an ethical approach so important to the teaching profession? Obviously because it is an inter-personal profession and clients have the right to feel able to rely on teachers to behave appropriately. Especially, it is important because the clients of teachers are young, even very young, people. Hence, the oft-heard statement that teachers are *in loco parentis*. The need for a Code stems in part from these factors; but also from the realisation that teachers – by definition – are in positions of power and influence; this power brings its own responsibilities. Teachers have been described as moral agents; that moral agency may be felt in a number of different ways. For example, the teacher as a role model may affect how students behave (see Chapters 3 and 10); or the teacher as a purveyor of knowledge may condition the student's mind and beliefs (see Chapter 4).

Ethical dilemmas are an everyday occurrence in the teaching context. Take a simple thing like playground duty in the primary sector. A teacher is on duty while the students let off steam. Inevitably six-year-old Johnny falls over and scrapes his knee quite badly. Johnny is in pain, and bleeding a bit, and is a bit shocked by the impact. Under the procedures for the school, however, the supervising teacher cannot pick Johnny up off the yard, dust him down a bit, say a few comforting words – because all this may be construed as 'inappropriate behaviour'. The supervisor has to stand over Johnny at a suitable distance, but send two reliable older pupils 100 metres away into the school building to find the qualified first aider, who will fetch their first aid kit, and proceed to join the teacher and Johnny, plaster the latter's leg and return to the building and fill in an accident form, while the apparently detached and uncaring supervisor gets on with his duty. Morality satisfied? Humanity sacrificed? Best obey the rules and stay safe!

The Professional Code for teachers assumes that teaching is a 'moral enterprise', i.e. both with respect to teachers' relationships with students and in their construction of learning experiences for them. These elements are characterised by care. But this simple picture is complicated by the prevalence of moral or ethical conflicts; typically, the competing interests of students, their parents and of the teachers themselves; possibly also, of the school, of politicians and of Society at large. Different teachers solve these moral conflicts in different ways according to their own 'moral context' in life and personal experience. Training, especially the use of case studies to draw out ethical literacy, may increase moral understanding for teachers but does not remove the range and depth of the dilemmas they face.

Furthermore, the individual teacher is not wholly in charge of the public perception of the profession and its ethical standards. Bad press when individual teachers commit serious breaches of the Code of Conduct taint the way in which Society sees all of us. In an example in Chapter 1, we talked about the principal whose appointment of a family member as the caretaker of a building purchased with academy money was called into question. If this behaviour is regarded as ethically questionable, then the general public may ask whether other staff in this 'questionably run' establishment are also part of the dubious morality, or even whether the students who go there have learned dubious ethical standards from their role models. Research within the business sector suggests that, when a company or organisation is led by a head who behaves with questionable ethics, this impacts over time on the employees, who ape their leader's behaviour; replacing the leader with one who is morally upright does not correct the situation. Concerned teachers need to uphold the Code for one reason above all: breaches of it impinge on us all.

THINKING THROUGH SCHOOL-BASED ETHICAL DILEMMAS

It seems appropriate, then, to draw this chapter to its close by setting out a few scenarios for ethical consideration. All of the incidents narrated here are based on actual situations. In each case, you will be asked about what you would do, and about your reasons.

Action

Read each scenario below, one at a time. In each case, answer the questions posed. Note that in every case the options for action are at least three or four in number.

Scenario 1

In your school, it is the tradition that the newest member of staff holds the tea-club finances which provide morning and afternoon drinks; any surplus gets used for cakes from time to time. The current treasurer, Glenda, is a probationer teacher who has only been in the profession for six months. You notice that the stocks of tea and coffee are a bit low, and that cakes never seem to feature on the agenda. Nor is there any petty cash in the usual tin. You know that Glenda's boyfriend has been made redundant and they are struggling for money. As Glenda's line manager, what options for action do you have? What are the ethical dilemmas which hedge around each of your options?

Scenario 2

In this scenario, you are an experienced member of staff in your sixth form college, the second in a child development vocational department; you are looking to move into running your own department. The principal of a neighbouring institution asks you if you will visit his school for a day's consultancy: he wants to satisfy himself about the quality of the work being done there. You are delighted with this because you know the department post is coming up in a few months, and you have set your sights on it.

You arrive at the host college and are met by the current head of the department, Mrs D. After some pleasantries, Mrs D says she will leave you with a student, Julie, who will show you to the rather distant training room where the next session will take place – Mrs D herself has to detour to fetch some equipment. Julie is a good host and a great advertisement for the course. When you get to the outlying area of the site, the previous class has not finished; the girls are waiting outside the room. A few moments later they all start to change their clothes in the corridor though male and female students are walking up and down the corridor. You ask Julie what is happening.

Apparently, when the students attend the child development sessions, they have to dress in a set uniform; as this area is so far from the main building and there are few facilities, they opt to change out of normal clothes in the corridor to save time. You observe the sessions for the child development programme, which are generally good. Now you have to present a report to the college principal about what you have observed, to make your judgement on it. What are you going to say in your report, given that you don't want to blot your copybook with the head in advance of the job advert? What ethical dilemmas underpin this scenario?

Scenario 3

You are in charge of a small group of staff. On Monday morning a hand-delivered letter is waiting for you. When you open it, you discover it is from a teacher in another school and concerns Michael, a member of your team. The other teacher, Mr W, was in the pub after a meeting on Saturday last, having a bar lunch. The local hostelry boasts those trendy, high-backed pews which shut off tables from one another and give privacy. He could, though, hear the conversation next door. Allegedly, Michael was sitting next door, oblivious of Mr W's presence, and bad-mouthing him in no uncertain terms to his mates. Mr W demands that you take action against Michael and write to him to explain what action has been undertaken. What options are open to you? What ethical dilemmas surround each of these options?

Scenario 4

As you check on the lesson preparation notes of members of your year-group you notice that one of your staff, Eric, is heavily reliant on the internet for planning. Eric is in his first year of teaching and sometimes struggles a bit, but potentially he is a good teacher. One particular piece of lesson preparation catches your eye. He is going to use some text with his students, but it is full of factual errors. These are obviously from the internet, but Eric has simply re-used the material without correction. What range of actions could you now take? What ethical considerations will you weigh up in each case?

3

THE ETHICAL SCHOOL'S APPROACH TO CLASS MANAGEMENT

STARTING TO ASSESS THE IMPORTANCE OF ETHICAL CONSCIOUSNESS IN SCHOOLS

When I was in America at an education conference, a delegate told this story. It's about a young teacher in a Wild West school in the 1800s (so a different culture, different era), trying to find his feet in the classroom. I've removed the Texan accent because it is hard to convey in print:

> The school was in an old barn with a few benches and not much equipment. Students came in on foot or on horse-back from outlying farms. They weren't the brightest buttons, but they were good kids. After about a week two new boys joined the class. They were older than the rest, built on a massive physical scale. They dwarfed me and made my life a living hell. Come Sunday I sat in church while the preacher was droning and thought about Monday morning, and I can tell you I was plum scared. On Monday I turned up and sure enough, those two haystacks came in shouting and hollering, and sat at the back heckling me. I walked down the barn about half way, and pulled my Colt from my belt. 'Next one says a word gets a slug', I announced. I never had no trouble after that.

Not a course of action to be emulated! Let's be clear about that: the vignette is not a route to follow. But this probably apocryphal incident has a serious message: there are plenty of young teachers (and some older ones) who will recognise the professional desolation in this tale. It is the negativity of that desolation I want to look at first. It is the cause of much stress, and issues in mental health problems for some.

I chose to become a teacher and, later, to work in some 'difficult' contexts; but – at my back – I had had a cautionary experience about professional desolation. As a pupil, I once watched my class decide to destroy a teacher – it was entirely calculated. He was a genial, experienced, to my mind fair, and physically imposing man; yet within the space of a lesson he had been reduced, first to tears, then to a total incapacity to act, begging children to respond. He walked out of the classroom, and never came back. He had used the skills he had; he possessed no other tools with which to manage. As a young teacher I resolved such an outcome would not happen to me. Surely, there is a better way?

I concluded that a better way was to adopt an ethical approach to class management. What exactly is an ethical school's approach to class management? We might make a first tentative definition something like:

> The intention of everyone in the school to espouse qualities like professionalism, integrity, honesty, respect and equality towards others. [These form the conceptual basis of the school's ethical stance.] The determination to behave towards one another in ways which exemplify these qualities – staff member to staff member, student to student, staff member to student, and student to staff member – at all times. [This puts into practice the conceptual ideals.]

This definition establishes some ethical principles. These principles may be codified and set into mission or values' statements. Such behaviour produces its own ethos. Implicit in this is the notion that ethical behaviour in schools begins from the top or with the members of staff (later we will come to student behaviour). First, an incident:

> An education consultant I knew once went into a school for a couple of days, following its rather dubious Ofsted Report, to do some training with staff. The school was in one of the worst areas in one of the more forgotten towns of the north of England – one of those places where a high spring tide in the North Sea

threatens to turn the institution into a newly independent fiefdom. It was, apparently, a surprisingly positive experience. The building itself was quite modern and practical enough; contrary to the local rumours, the kids caught her pleasantly unawares with their overall levels of politeness and a willingness to chat over lunch or at other times; staff generally felt that they wanted advice and were certainly open to ideas to a degree that is not always apparent. For two days she wandered purposefully around the school and enjoyed all the contacts she made – and the only person she didn't meet was the principal.

When the formal training was over and her work done, the deputy said to her: 'You had better say good-bye to the principal'; she led my acquaintance on a long and tortuous route, upstairs and along corridors in deserted places she hadn't yet explored. At the end of an upper corridor was a short flight of steps down into a self-contained mezzanine level (the journey was like something out of the 2010 horror film, The Maze). Ahead was a solid wooden door, with a notice securely welded to it. She was sure the message didn't actually read: **No entry to anybody, at any time, on any pretext.** But it might as well have done. The door did not yield to normal attempts to open it.

The deputy looked at her apologetically: 'I'm sorry for the wild goose chase', she said. 'I think he must have gone home'. Then, as an afterthought: 'When he's here he never comes out of the office, the door is always locked like this'.

The school failed its follow-up Ofsted assessment: something to do with failed leadership of the senior management team!

Clearly, for whatever reason, ethical qualities such as those which were defined at the start of this chapter did not operate from the top down in this school: the principal did not share them with the staff, any more than he had shared their training experiences. I began this chapter by thinking about a principal to illustrate, simply, that ethos and ethics often begin there; and have a hard time permeating down the structure if they go missing. In this instance you will have deduced that the rest of the Senior Leadership Team (SLT) had made a pretty good job of running the school in the absence of leadership from the very top. Let me also add that, from visiting thousands of schools across many countries, such a situation is very rare.

REFLECTION ON ETHICAL CONSCIOUSNESS IN SCHOOL

The first step on the way to an ethically run school is to have teachers who see themselves as ethical beings, who adopt a personal code of ethics, and who apply that to the management of their classroom and leadership work. This realisation does not have to be detailed and profound, it just needs some guiding principles:

- Ethical conduct towards students
- Ethical conduct relating to learning practices and teacher performance
- Ethical conduct towards one's professional colleagues
- Ethical conduct to parents and the whole school community

> **Action**
>
> Maybe this is the moment to take stock of your own school and of your own department or faculty. Be challenging: ask yourself honestly what kind of an institution you work in. There will almost certainly be good and bad aspects; hopefully, the good will far outweigh the bad as they do in most schools. But there is always room for improvement. Using the four bullet-points above, write a strengths and weaknesses list for your school and/or your department or a school which you have worked in. Of course, keep your thoughts confidential and anonymised – they are only for your use. Try to deduce the ethical principles your chosen school adopts. If it encodes these into a public statement, assess to what extent they succeed.

ETHICS AND ETHOS

Every school conveys its own atmosphere: to an experienced nose it's as obvious on entering the building as the smell of school dinners. It is this atmosphere which emanates from the school's overall mission statement and statement of values; I prefer the word ethos to describe it. This ethos underpins relationships in the school; it determines how members of the school behave to one another and – among other things – the way in which the school itself, and classes within it, are managed.

This ethos gets translated down through the structural layers of the school. So groups – faculties, departments, tutor groups, team teaching units, houses for games where they still exist and so on – take on the fundamental ethos of the school but adapt it to their own environments and purposes; in sport for example, in the way in which they play the game, and way in which they treat visiting teams.

Finally, the ethos is relayed to the classroom level: to the way in which individual teachers operate and the ways in which students respond to these teachers. New teachers coming into a situation find they must create their own personal version of this ethos, absorb and become part of it; substitute teachers on supply sometimes struggle to control someone else's class, which is otherwise tractable. I have done some supply work: in certain locations where school ethos is poor, it can be an alienating experience.

Generally, then, one would expect the overall ethos of the school to arise out of the aspirations of the Senior Leadership Team, to be critical to its success, and to operate on the ethical principles the school espouses. Ethos is intimately related to how schools answer the ethical problems with which the business of education presents them. The school's overall ethos and ethical approach determine how class management works within the school; since there can be no meaningful learning without sensible discipline and self-discipline, this is a crucial matter. Good management begins with how students behave around the school as a whole, but these ethically-based standards then get applied in the other layers, too, with adaptations: at the level of management of the sub-units like departments, as well as in individual classes. So this chapter takes a first look at these three layers in turn in an attempt to de-construct how they work and what effects they have on students and staff in the management of the school. The theme of how to create an effective and positive ethos which then rubs off into positive behaviour in individual students is picked up again later in the chapter.

How can we sum up what whole school ethos has to do with ethics? Put simplistically, the answer to the question goes like this:

For a Society to exist productively, it needs to articulate and share its values and intentions, and for its citizens to live these in their day-to-day lives. A school is a society in miniature: it, too, needs to identify its mission, values, intentions, aspirations – and these, in turn, need to be shared by the members of the school for the school society to work smoothly and flourish. Ethics – as the philosophy and rationale underlying the code of values on which a society or school operates (see Chapter 1) – underpin the rationale which inform the school's ethos and result from it.

Most schools will formulate their values by talking about keeping students safe, making them feel included, fostering respect and valuing each individual. Staff–student relations will be positive; a secure learning climate will be created; and the contributions of all will be welcome. There is increasing emphasis on well-being: one Scottish document [1] puts it like this:

> 'Climate' and ethos are key determinants in promoting social and emotional wellbeing and mental health for all in schools. This is described as 'core values, attitudes, beliefs and culture of the school and classroom' and includes school 'connectedness' and a feeling of being accepted, respected and bonded to the school environment. School climate can also be seen as incorporating three essential aspects – engagement, safety and environment. These aspects are seen as essential to maintaining positive relationships and social and emotional wellbeing.

The school's ethos will attempt to lay the ground rules or ethical guidelines for how students behave to one another, and for staff–student relations. Almost every school will sign up to honest dealings, mutual respect, good manners, calm and controlled behaviour. There's a kind of notion implicit here of 'we're all in this together' – everyone must play a part, preferably a part in tune with the same ideals. The adopted ethos of any particular school may vary marginally from the school next door: for example, a faith school might differ from a secular school; or a school with close associations with the military (often fee-paying schools) may have a particular stance which reflects this interest. But, in general, we can expect many overlaps. An ethical school is likely then to demonstrate these characteristics:

- Staff behave fully in line with their professional codes of conduct (see Chapter 2)
- All members of the school community behave with honesty, integrity, truthfulness and consideration for others

- Students behave in ways which exhibit respect, to each other and towards staff members
- Specific behaviours may be outlawed (for example, bad language, interrupting others, shouting, not paying attention, not bringing required equipment to lessons)
- All members of the school community adopt positive standards of support for one another and for the school as a whole.

There will be others of a similar kind, which may vary slightly but which pursue similar intentions.

> **Action**
>
> In the previous ACTION you considered a list of your chosen school's strengths and weaknesses, and its roots in ethical principles. In the light of the discussion above, pause to think about staff members specifically, and how they work together positively to contribute to the ethos of the school and the effective management of student behaviour. How do staff members (teachers and non-teaching staff) put into practice the vision, mission and ethical intentions of the school? What good qualities might you extrapolate from your school to recommend to others?

ETHICS AND SANCTIONS

If schools are societies in miniature, then we have to remember that in public life, those who fail to live up to the values of Society are subject to sanctions. A good example relates to the coronavirus outbreak in 2020 when the public was on 'lockdown' in their homes. Though we cannot comment on its accuracy, this is the bare bones of how the BBC [2] ran the story:

- A medical officer resigned after making two trips to a second home during the coronavirus lockdown. The officer subsequently apologised, and planned to continue in the role
- The officer had received a police warning for breaking the lockdown rules after newspaper photographs taken of this individual visiting a location more than an hour's drive from the main family home

- The officer had been the public face of media adverts urging the public to stay at home to save lives
- Later, a statement was released indicating resignation.

The same kinds of sanctions apply to schools. They apply not only to students but to staff members; and must begin there if students are to respect the ethics of the school community. It is always disappointing, in life and in school, when a senior person falls from grace. It is very unfortunate when the incident is one which is perhaps a momentary aberration and wholly untypical; one's sympathy level drops exponentially when the culpable act is delivered in cold blood and with intent. There have been, for example, a number of cases relating to alleged manipulation of SATs results. This is a generic example:

> A head teacher was suspended for allegedly tampering with the annual SATs test papers. At the end of the testing these papers were left in his (apparently unlocked) room, on his desk. Subsequently, it was discovered that many of the students' answers had been altered; some of the alterations were rather clumsy. An immediate investigation concluded that evidence pointed to the head teacher. At a later tribunal, however, the tribunal chairperson agreed that the evidence of location of the papers when the alterations were discovered was only circumstantial in pointing the finger of blame at the head. Multiple alterations had been made; but the alterations were not consistent in style and appeared to have been by several hands. There were suggestions of a vendetta against the head by a group of staff members, but there was nothing to link them to the cheating. The head was cleared of wrongdoing. Had that not been the case, he would have been dismissed.

Nevertheless, cases of this kind raise some interesting issues about the failure of school ethos and the ethical standards on which this is based. In the instance quoted, questions might need to be asked. In interrogating this incident, we might need to ask:

- What were the school's normal procedures for security? What were the access arrangements in respect of these papers? Were

they adequate? Were they followed? Were there any loopholes? What do security arrangements in this school tell us about this educational community?
- When the test papers were collected and located in the head's room, who had access and for what purpose? Did the arrangements protect the students by protecting their test papers?
- It was alleged that individual test papers were altered and by more than one person. What might have been the motivation for this unprofessional act?
- What were the intended and unforeseen consequences of this act? Was it a fear of poor results? An attempt to make the school, a teacher/s look better? An attempt to advantage/disadvantage certain students? Nothing to do with students? A staff vendetta? By whom? Against whom? Did it have unintended consequences for students and what were they? Did it have consequences for 'interested others', e.g. parents? What were these?
- What outcomes did it have for the school? How did it affect the reputation of the school? Of staff members, whether involved or not? Of students exiting this school into other community schools? Of school governors ... and so on?
- The ethical dimensions of this incident cannot be fully appreciated without knowing the answers to all these questions and more; but we do not know them, so our understanding of the situation is partial and our analysis curtailed. So, as often, our final interrogation should be: What do we need to know, that we don't know, in order to make the best possible judgement about this incident?

What we can say is: the reputation of the school was damaged and trust at all levels compromised. The ill-judged act of dishonesty, possibly by several people, had blown out of the water any attempt to set an example to students about ethical behaviour: though no perpetrators were discovered and disciplined, the whole declared ethical rationale of the school was called into question. By interrogating this incident in the way described above, we may gain a better understanding of how and why individuals may subvert the ethical principles on which a school runs.

> **Action**
>
> Breaking the management or behavioural codes of the school will incur a sanction. For the moment, let us confine our thoughts to students who break the rules. What are the policies which operate in your school when students step out of line? How clearly are they articulated to both students and staff? From your experience, are these policies effective? When (if at all) are they not effective? If they fail, why do they fail? Do the students see these school policies as just? Weigh the sanctions' policies against these criteria:
>
> - Are they proportionate?
> - Are they fairly applied?
> - Do they discriminate in any way?
> - Are they appropriate to the socio-economic context of the school?

Formulating the overall intended ethos for any school, from the top down, and the ethical rationale on which this is based, is the business, fundamentally, of the Senior Management Team: the application of it falls on middle leaders and individual staff members to whom we now turn.

CLASSROOM BEHAVIOUR: THE NEED FOR AN ETHICAL APPROACH

If I enter a school which I have never visited before, I always enjoy seeing those where the school plant allows faculties or departments to be grouped together rather than having their work scattered around the building. It always feels good to be immersed in French or Spanish phrases in a modern languages department or surrounded by beautiful pieces of art or designed objects in a technology area. The ethos of such areas will usually be down to the middle leadership of the school and will exemplify how they relate to the school's mission and ideals. However, though the faculty or department may make a big effort with their subject-related activity, Ofsted, in a 2013 survey of low-level disruption [3], nonetheless holds that middle leaders are culpable at times of neglecting the wider behavioural issues.

More than 50% of teachers surveyed by Ofsted claimed that their school's policy on behaviour was helpful in itself; yet they claimed it was inconsistently applied across the school. In some instances, teaching staff found that discipline was undermined by the inconsistent approach of other teaching staff to behaviour. Though it is tempting just to blame senior leaders for this, the position isn't tenable. Senior leaders can set standards and enforce them around the school plant, but teachers must accept individual responsibility; to do this, they need the support of middle leaders to help enforce the school's policies at all times.

If the school's ethical aspirations and intentions are for polite, respectful behaviour between students, and towards teachers, then classes cannot be dominated by low level disruption: it is not tolerable for students to shout one another down, interrupt, call one another names, interrupt the teacher, disturb other people's work and so on. For this reason, most worrying of all in the Ofsted findings was that a significant proportion of teachers thought that low level disruption had little negative effect on students' learning, even though they also believed it accounted for a massive loss of learning time: this is simply not logical. There is no doubt that learning time is a critical factor in effective learning.

Professional colleagues have a professional obligation to support the school mission and ethos: to be a cog in the wheel of school discipline not to be a spanner in its works. Ethically, every teacher owes it to every colleague. I can recall in my own career an instance of this. My opposite number used to teach a friendly, but lively, class second period after lunch on a Tuesday – he taught them at other times and they were fine, but on Tuesdays they came noisy, boisterous and disruptive. The key factor was the teacher who preceded his lesson: she allowed a mild degree of bedlam to permeate all her lessons. His attempts to talk to senior staff fell on deaf ears; he was forced, in the end, to confront the class. He told them how good they were at other times, but on Tuesdays they showed a different personality. He had to explain that the norms of Mrs X were neither the norms of the school nor the norms that he followed. His action was born out of inexperience, and probably ethically questionable – yet it was an act of self-preservation (and it worked). In ethical terms, though, there might be another thought to add: Mrs X had been in the profession long enough to have learned better class management skills; her teaching style was participatory (good, in itself), but she could not then control the exuberance of students, in this challenging school, which she had encouraged. The result was that she herself was more stressed than she needed to be – the constant bedlam of her classroom must have been very wearing and put her own mental health at risk. The SLT might have been more proactive in taking control of this situation and protecting her from herself.

TEACHERS UPHOLDING THE ETHICAL STANDARDS OF THE SCHOOL

At the personal level, everyone who works in classrooms – teachers and non-teaching assistants – must share a set of personal standards; these are derived from the kinds of qualities embedded in most schools' mission and vision statements; they are the ethical principles on which the school bases its ethos, for example:

- **Impartiality** – a scrupulous approach to equality at all times
- **Respect** – for everyone in the class and the school, or who visits the school
- **Patience** – avoiding irritation when students find things hard
- **Concern** – which includes knowing students well, and moulding one's own behaviour appropriately
- **Integrity** – always being honest with one's self and with others regardless of their role in the school
- **Propriety** – students will role-model on you: be worthy in your behaviour.

The classroom is a learning environment: it teaches educational and social habits from the moment students enter. The teacher is one part of social learning – the students themselves form another part: their relationships and interactions, how they do their work, how they set about completing tasks. The persons most involved in all these things are the students, so they need some control over their learning experiences. But a part of that experience is their guide: the teacher.

At the level of the classroom teacher (whether he/she holds a leadership post or not), the school's values are lived out face-to-face with students and among the processes of their learning. Here, the grand resolutions bear fruit or turn to dust. I am often amused by the opinions about teaching from those who have never stood in front of a sea of classroom faces. Some think it's easy, they say 'can't see what all the fuss is about'. Others go weak at the knees – a feeling that may be shared by trainee or probationer teachers, and which is nicely captured by Penelope Fitzgerald [4] describing a young teacher putting the next day's work on the board so she didn't have to turn her back on the class. Turning one's back on children was as unwise as in lion taming, she declared.

Fitzgerald, though – despite her humorous turn of phrase – was brought up in the cloistered privilege of a bishop's palace, attended a private school and Oxford, and was never, as far as I know, a teacher. Teachers generally understand that most students do not have a privileged background; and they know, too, that many factors can lead to power struggles in the classroom which require management skills. As teachers, we have to acknowledge that our first concern is the well-being of all children, to accept the fact that some children don't achieve or behave in challenging ways. But we need to give them the opportunity to learn, too. So, despite Fitzgerald's humour, I am far more persuaded by Haim Ginott [5], who was himself a teacher. His view has the perceptiveness of experience:

> I've come to a frightening conclusion that I am the decisive element in the classroom. It's my personal approach that creates the climate. It's my daily mood that makes the weather. As a teacher, I possess a tremendous power to make a child's life miserable or joyous. I can be a tool of torture or an instrument of inspiration. I can humiliate or heal. In all situations, it is my response that decides whether a crisis will be escalated or de-escalated and a child humanised or dehumanised.

Action

Ginott's quotation, above, is a very telling one. Jot down some notes about how this works in your classroom. From your deliberations with yourself, challenge yourself to see whether your behaviour might be modified in order to help student behaviour and attitudes to change for the better too. [Trainee teachers might think about the work of a teacher they admire and might model on.]

Though guided by the school's vision of its intentions, the individual teacher remains godlike within the four walls of the classroom – which I once likened to Andrew Marvell's [6] description of the grave. For this reason above all others, the teacher is entrusted with a dread responsibility: that of helping each child to fulfil their potential within a safe and inviting environment. The status a teacher has means that he/she must behave in a manner which upholds the ethical intentions of the school; he/she is a role model and without that guidance how can students be expected to absorb, learn and put into practice their personal ethical behaviours?

ETHICAL APPROACHES TO CLASS MANAGEMENT

When it comes to the act of controlling the behaviour of a class, there's plenty of simplistic advice around about class management – what works and what doesn't; and there is some sound counsel as well – and you should consult this. The present textbook is not concerned with the myriad individual skills of class management, but with the bigger questions of ethical policy (which must, later, be translated into individual actions). But it is true that students have the capacity to disrupt; and teachers have an obligation to keep all students on-board with learning which is not disrupted.

All the handy manuals of class management will provide lists of low-level disruption; and most will tell you that these acts are far more frequent and annoying than an occasional piece of off-the-wall unacceptable behaviour. Low level disruption consists typically of:

- Chat with other students which is off-task and not relevant to the work in hand
- Showing a lack of respect for other students, e.g. talking over them, interrupting
- Showing a lack of respect for staff, e.g. challenging their instructions or speaking in a rude manner
- Calling out without permission
- Deliberately failing to bring books, equipment or other requisites
- Bringing irrelevant articles into class – from mobiles to toys
- Pretending not to be able to follow instructions or start a task

- Eating or drinking at inappropriate times
- Intentionally disturbing other students who are on-task
- Using bad language.

These can be very hard issues to tackle, especially if the learning environment itself is not good, e.g. where students work in overheated rooms, or are unsighted by sunlight when window blinds are inadequate; where floors are hard-surfaced and chairs make a constant scraping noise; where the view from the window is particularly distracting; when teachers fail to open windows and classrooms get stuffy; when weather is inimical (hot, wet, stuffy, windy). The teacher has, at some point, to enter into a 'contract' with students about what is, and what is not, acceptable behaviour – and the students need to own the decision, so it helps if they make the rules. Unacceptable behaviour is not always malicious in intent but it can still be very disruptive, as the following incident, recounted to me by one of my fellow trainers, shows:

> One of my favourite examples concerned a very able young teacher who went to teach a well-behaved class and found her lesson disrupted, not by any action from the students, but simply by her own instinct that 'something' was wrong. She did the usual checks: glanced round to ensure people were sitting in their allotted places, no-one was missing, there were no scuffles under desks, no notes being passed. She reported that her lesson gradually fell apart because of her uncomfortable feeling. Then the penny dropped. Four girls always sat in a line in the front row: they were all there, and all in the usual order. They were all wearing their spectacles – which they all legitimately wore. They had just simply swapped glasses! The teacher's instinct was right; the disruption, though, was significant, even though none of the students stepped out of line. Though it was clever, and quite droll, the four girls were still transgressing the intentions of the school's ethos and code of ethics.

Of course, students can commit much more serious breaches of the school's intended vision, acts which definitely offend the school's and society's ethical codes; in some senses, these are easier to decide about as they may also offend, e.g., against society's norms or even the law of the land. Two examples of this will suffice. In the first, a student defecated in the school hall under the school's stage. The offence became obvious after a day or two; those with the potential to commit the offence were narrowed down to one class and the culprit was identified because he had boasted about it to putative friends who were scandalised by his action. The second case concerned students creeping back to the building after hours and setting fire to a laboratory; the students had intended it as a prank against a specific teacher, but unfortunately the ageing window blinds went up in flames and significant damage was caused to the whole teaching block. In the end, this action harmed a lot of people, both teachers and students.

TEACHERS' ETHICAL DILEMMAS IN SCHOOL

Orly Shapra-Lishchinsky [7] investigated examples of ethical conflict among trainee teachers. Their inexperience tended to make these beginning teachers open to dilemmas which pitted their students' actions against the rigidity of school precepts. Trainee teachers were persuaded to act inappropriately when they felt students needed care rather than school rules; they contrasted fair outcomes from punishment for misdemeanours (as they saw them) with the harshness of school rules. They found matters of confidentiality tough to deal with within the rules; and were persuaded towards loyalty to teaching colleagues rather than the school's formal systems. Especially difficult for them was when the families of students put pressure on them to act against normal school policy (though, in British schools, such situations should never arise – trainees would not usually deal with parents directly).

How teachers deal ethically with class management issues that arise might have to take on:

- A greater reliance on advice from middle and senior managers
- A recognition that things learned from students are not 'under the seal of the confessional'; in cases such as law breaking or danger to the student, help must be sought from appropriate quarters
- The closer age gap between older students and the youngest teachers cannot be allowed to sway professional behaviour

- Teachers, like probation officers and other caring professionals, must be able to distance themselves emotionally from their student clients
- Teachers need to take seriously their duty of care, but accept that they do not 'own' students and must allow appropriate others with more experience to advise
- Above all, they must be seen to pursue their work without fear or favour, in a spirit of fairness to all students and within the ideals of equality for all.

DEBATING AN ETHICAL ISSUE

Here's a puzzle to end on (you might want to look back to the three scenarios at the end of Chapter 1 to start off your thinking):

> A large secondary school SLT made the decision that students were coming to school in hairstyles which were too unconventional. It therefore set about banning those which it considered unacceptable, even producing an on-line set of examples of what would not be tolerated. Some of the outlawed styles involved excessively short and/or excessively long hair; most of the styles were modelled on those of current celebrities. The school's action upset a lot of students and some parents, causing a backlash against the school in the Press. Staff at the school were divided on the issue.

Action

In a staff meeting or in a faculty meeting (take the role of teacher or of middle leader as appropriate), how would you debate this issue from an ethical perspective? Generate a set of questions which staff might discuss in order to reveal the ethical issues at stake here, e.g. how does the rule relate to personal freedom? On what basis of authority does a school act in cases like this?

There is one key insight (to be pursued in the following chapters) which will get ethical class management and a good learning ethos off on the right foot, and it's really simple to say (it may be harder to do, but not impossible otherwise you wouldn't be a teacher): **make lessons interesting.** Let the students' enthusiasm be not for inventive disruption but for active participation. I like John Dewey's [8] insight:

> If you have an end in view of ... children learning certain set lessons, to be recited to a teacher, your discipline must be devoted to securing that result. But if the end in view is the development of a spirit of social co-operation and community life, discipline must grow out of and be relative to such an aim.

4

ETHICAL CURRICULUM

MAKING A CURRICULUM ETHICAL

Andrew O'Hagan [9], in his novel *Be Near Me*, has his schoolmaster rail against the curriculum: he talked about Pugin and Byrd instead.

I laughed when I read this: one teacher I knew as a teenager always shoehorned the English curriculum into four of its five allotted periods a week so that he could arraign us in the remaining time with his insights into the Dutch master painters, illustrated with numerous photographs from the National Gallery and elsewhere – at one level, I wasn't very interested, yet I learned a lot and gained an appreciation of how to look at art. Maybe, if you have some raging passion for a particular topic, you have been tempted into not dissimilar subterfuge.

Beyond the whole curriculum, individual subject areas don't always fare well in literature either; one suspects that writers – who as children could not vent their frustrations on their teachers – get their own back by exposing them to their readers at a later date. Mavis Cheek [10] seems to fall into this genre with this gem about the fact-based history we all knew and hated as children: history has the last laugh by being conjecture and interpretation.

Even closer to the truth, in my view, is the French author and historian, Hyppolyte Taine [11], who opines:

An English head ... contains many facts and few ideas.

That might almost be the theme of this chapter, and the next. Taking this as the clue, what might be included in a set of principles for an ethical curriculum and how it is delivered? Curriculum is about content, about those elements which are extra to the formal curriculum content, and about how these things are delivered, i.e. associated pedagogy.

I suggest, then, that ethical curriculum content might conform to conceptual requirements such as:

- Accuracy
- Truthfulness
- Fairness
- Balance
- Breadth
- Usefulness
- Transferability.

If I were to challenge a room full of teachers to list six key descriptors of an ethical curriculum, then the following would feature frequently in their responses:

- Content which fitted learners for life: intellectually, for employment and for leisure
- Content which fulfilled the main intentions of education: knowledge, skills and understanding
- Content which was honest, truthful and reliable
- Content that led to attitudes and habits which were socially productive – e.g. concern for others and empathy
- Values' education: integrity, courage, honesty, etc.
- Education of the self: self-image, realism, inter-personal relationships, etc.

Every consideration of curriculum needs to be measured against yardsticks such as these. The issue for teachers is whether the curriculum which they are required to teach meshes with these fundamental principles.

Ethical curriculum content, beyond the formal or prescribed, might seek to supplement the formal with:

- Desirable attitudes
- Interest and commitment to learning

- Wider dimensions of involvement or understanding
- Broader experiences
- Application of knowledge and understanding
- Relevance to life, employment and productive leisure.

Both of these contents might imply ethical approaches as to how they are presented, i.e. to pedagogy:

- High quality and varied learning experiences
- Unbiased approaches
- Integrity in presentation
- Student participation in their own learning
- A degree of student control.

This chapter is mainly about curriculum content and pedagogy will be mentioned to provide some context, but will not be dealt with at length until Chapter 5.

When I came to write this chapter one commentator claimed that the English education system was 'deregulated' and 'autonomous'. In the current situation, nothing could be further from the truth! The English curriculum is regulated by the provision of the National Curriculum; and – although schools are frequently told by Ofsted that they don't have to follow this in detail – schools which want to break free are neither actively encouraged nor can escape having to make a very strong case for stepping out of line. Although those responsible would claim that they take professional advice, the National Curriculum is substantially the result of decisions by civil servants and politicians: it emanates from a Government Department.

During the Covid 19 lockdown, some teachers trawled Ofsted reports to see what they said about curriculum, and discovered the usual indecisiveness and prevarication on the issue of curriculum building. The value of a planned and sequenced curriculum featured in Ofsted thinking; this involved identifying the knowledge and skills (but interestingly, not the understanding) which teachers expect from a specific subject and a specific year group. School leaders were expected to make links between subjects; and teachers were expected to connect new knowledge with old; but interdisciplinary approaches and their educational value were ignored. It was acknowledged that planning and sequencing across subjects and years was a demanding undertaking. So as always, Ofsted sat on the fence, asking for all things to all students but giving little actual guidance. The omission of 'understanding' is also a key here: it suggests the centrality of the information approach of the 'facts and dates' school of learning, rather than the more intellectual approach of thinking and critical analysis. This kind of 'slip of the tongue' speaks with louder volume than words do.

There was also some interesting public dialogue between teachers about curriculum, which I felt hit the mark. To paraphrase: Teacher A said she was tired of the Covid debate about how much learning students were missing, and pointed out that most had probably learned a great deal and very valuable material during lockdown. Teacher B, though, nailed the issue by objecting – saying that communicating that material is not what teachers are assessed on. There is a perception in the profession – which I believe to be accurate – that, despite the official guidance often feeling unspecific, there is a requirement and expectation that teachers will teach a defined body of knowledge (and, implicitly, that any knowledge outside this domain is regarded as either irrelevant or not useful).

But I want you to imagine for a short while at the start of the chapter that it is possible to have a blank canvas. Only by doing this, will one be able to ask the right questions. So, I want to take you back to a time when curriculum was genuinely deregulated, and when there were – as a result – lively curriculum debates. Not, that is, debates about the detail of choices to be made within the pre-defined content, but real questions about of what curriculum should consist, and how, given freedom of choice, it could best be delivered to the advantage of all students.

To do this I am going to take you back to a writer on curriculum called Lawrence Stenhouse. The fact that his work was carried out some decades ago does not make it either 'dated' or 'irrelevant'. The discussion of Stenhouse is not about content (which could be dated), but about principles (which are not). It was carried through at a time when genuinely open discussion was possible, and thus it allows us to have that open debate. But first, please use the ACTION below to do a bit of thinking for yourself.

> **Action**
>
> Consider for a moment where the current curricula which you teach come from. Make a list of the answers (there will be more than one). On what ethical principles is this curriculum predicated? Using the knowledge you have gained so far in this text, try to identify what it is that makes your curriculum ethical. What doubts, if any, do you have about it from an ethical perspective?

AN EXEMPLARY APPROACH TO ETHICAL CURRICULUM

We have seen, the curriculum in today's UK schools is largely the domain of Government, which in turn means of civil servants under the guidance of elected politicians who may (or may not) have specific axes to grind on the whet-stone of dogma. But it was not always thus – so I am beginning this chapter from an ancient world (actually the 1970s – so before more than half the teaching force was born), when curriculum innovation ruled OK.

Perhaps the greatest education guru of the age (at least in terms of his innovative curriculum content and how this was delivered) was Lawrence Stenhouse [12], who headed up a Government-funded project known as the Humanities Curriculum Project (HCP). It was one of the most significant innovations of its time, though for reasons which will emerge, it did not have the enduring influence it deserved.

So what was important about HCP? It had three main pillars:

Pillar 1: **An underlying philosophy** that the teacher had a duty to present materials to students (in this case secondary students – but the ideas are totally transferable to younger and older age groups) which balance the picture they paint in ways which are fair. For the moment, let's take a relatively fatuous example (so that we don't get involved too deeply in tangents about educational sacred cows): suppose we want to teach material about the use of public roads. This is a controversial issue and would have to look at the protagonists in the debate – these would be, most obviously, car drivers, heavy goods vehicle drivers and (motor)cyclists. A fair approach would be to look at the key arguments of each stakeholder – so, the high road taxes charged to motorists or the green credentials of cyclists. But then we would discover another level of debate: problems of providing appropriate infra-structure for cyclists, or the notion of 'penalty' for using allegedly polluting fuels, the social usefulness of road haulage, electric vehicles. Then there are other stakeholders – pedestrians, the police – and other issues, such as engineering for safe road and vehicle use, the pros and cons of 'black-box' recorders and so on. There are examples from other countries – and how they tackle these shared issues (and why they operate differently, perhaps). To examine the issue fairly, we have both to explore wider and delve deeper. This subject – and all topics worthy of consideration – are multi-layered and can be explored with increasing knowledge and insight.

Perhaps, at this point, it is worth pointing out the extreme opposite of what Stenhouse is saying. A teacher who consistently uses materials (i.e. curriculum content) which is biased and presents only his/her own views of an argument or situation, and who compounds that bias by skewing their teaching to promote these personal and unbalanced views, is guilty of indoctrination. Neither curriculum nor pedagogy can be ethically sound if it is biased and closed from alternative viewpoint.

Pillar 2: **A (starter) bank of materials** that will resource this debate. These result from the need for the teacher, and students, to have access to (or to discover as they pursue the topic) a range of support materials which will feed open and enquiring minds across the whole range of issues (eventually, any commercial materials will probably run out, and fresh tangents will require both teacher and students to find their own to follow the trail of enquiry. This process could be even more efficient than Stenhouse envisaged in an e-world of information). Curriculum building becomes not so much an exact science, but a diverse and inventive one.

Pillar 3: **A suitable methodology for teaching.** To deliver this curriculum the teacher needs a suitable methodology, one which fits the nature of the material and the classroom activity. Since the material is based on an issue, a problem or a debate, so the teaching method becomes one of enquiry, searching for evidence, asking deeper questions, not taking statements at face value, plus class discussion to which everyone (teacher and students) needs to contribute. Pillar 3 is included here for context; it will be discussed in the next chapter.

I am tempted to label these three foundations of learning Stenhouse's Three Pillars of Wisdom (definitely not a phrase he ever used). I believe that Stenhouse's curriculum approach also embodies a fundamental truth which, as far as I am aware, he never articulates in quite this way, and it is this. Generally speaking, curriculum as taught to students in schools (maybe even to students in colleges and universities) is largely imposed – by the government, Society, influenced by learned societies or by teachers themselves. By contrast, what Stenhouse strives for is a curriculum owned – at least in significant part – by students themselves. In his system, it is students who control, to some degree, both the direction of learning travel and – by definition – the content examined. This is a significant insight. It is picked up again later in this book (in Chapter 5) in the discussion of the teaching approach known as heutagogy. For the moment, let us simply put down a marker that, for a curriculum to be ethical, it must be co-owned by the learners not imposed by the teachers.

ETHICAL CURRICULUM AND THE NATIONAL CURRICULUM

Now, contrast this with the National Curriculum. Ostensibly a national minimum entitlement (a good thing), it is in fact a national syllabus (a more debatable thing) – more debatable because we have to ask: whose decision is this content, and does it exclude bias and dogma? Then add the interpretation put on this Curriculum by at least some politicians (e.g. 'we should all learn certain key facts of history'). But the so-called facts are open to debate and interpretation – so whose interpretation are we supposed to be learning? And then there's the real killer: examinations – which require the 'right' answers to be tested and rewarded, and whose syllabuses ring-fence what are, and what are not, preferred topics for learning. Room for innovation is limited, and methodology is likely to veer to the didactic (how many teachers in primary and secondary schools have we heard say the dreaded words: 'We have to get through the syllabus by April'? – It's no better than tourists on a coach outing having to 'do' York Minster before breakfast.)

> **Action**
>
> How free are you to adapt and refine the curriculum which you teach? Do students find it interesting? If not, why not? If you could, how would you change it?

CURRICULA ACROSS THE SCHOOL: AN ETHICAL PERSPECTIVE

But you might be saying at this point – 'So what! Your earlier example above is just a debate about cyclists and motorists. Not very relevant'. But the issue isn't about road usage, is it? It's a debate about:

History: A class is studying the history of WW2. It needs, of course, to look at the causes, the dates, the nations involved and the main actors in the drama. But to understand the War, students also have to feel an empathy – e.g. towards the era: they may talk to people who lived through it, listen to popular music of the time, visit an aviation museum. They will, of course, learn who won. But it is questionable to what extent the students will explore in depth the bigger questions: will they look at the same incident(s) – maybe the Dams raid – from the perspective of both the victors and the vanquished? Will they face the experience of rationing or hunger (and how might they do this?) Could they explore the psychology of mass rallies and how they might cloud a person's judgement? Will they ask what it was like to be a prisoner (a British prisoner in Stalag luft 3; a German prisoner in North Yorkshire). Learning dates and 'facts' is impoverished history: you can test it, but it is worth testing? Will the students consider the central issue: can war ever be right, and if so, under what circumstances?

Geography: This is a subject which has improved in leaps and bounds over recent years. It tends to be concerned with human, economic and environmental issues as part of the study, and has abandoned its somewhat stuffy image as 'looking at maps and learning about countries'. There is a good deal of practical work, and amongst this are skills for life. But at General Certificate of Secondary Education(GCSE) level, anyway, questions might be raised about how insightfully the subject is assessed. Multi-choice questions used in some instances are a mechanistic means of gaining insight into a student's knowledge. Geography is definitely at an advantage, potentially, in its ability to exploit the great outdoors at home and abroad. Many of these opportunities are available to students; their quality depends upon how well they are set up with learning intentions which are then fulfilled.

Religion: As a former teacher educator, I have sat through many RE lessons and even more assemblies. One of the things that strikes me during RE lessons is how infrequently they ask ultimate questions. I watched one of the (putatively) best RE teachers in a Local Authority over an extended period of time to discover what were her secrets which enabled this reputation. She presented quite interesting historical material about Judaism, Christianity and even other faiths; but I never saw her ask her secondary students to consider the fundamental claims of a faith. Even less likely, it seemed, was anything which might reflect on that other face of religious history – narrow-mindedness, intolerance, bigotry, sectarian violence or political shenanigans – from the witch doctor's control of a tribe to Henry VIII's fabricated divorces. The safe option is always: when the questions get tough, build a model of a church, temple, or other edifice, or decorate the classroom walls with faith symbols.

English Literature: The radio programme Desert Island Discs is still going after more than 70 years; at the end, the castaway is told they can have copies of the Bible and Shakespeare to help fill their isolated lives. Both volumes are mini-libraries and would consume a lot of time to absorb, but the choice seems oddly anachronistic: only a minority of the British population are active Christians; and Shakespeare, as a 16th century writer who may, or may not, have authored some or all of the alleged works attributed to him, may not be the most representative (let alone 'best') writer to exemplify English literature. Any choice is likely to be controversial – Dickens, Brontë, Austen and Wells inevitably – but also more 'modern' authors, many of whom are not actually all that modern. Every time the examination boards make changes to their syllabi, there is a contention about exactly what can be considered worthy of inclusion in those formative texts which are inflicted on groups of teenagers taking tests in them. But this might not be the worst aspect of the problem: the internet and hard copy publishers now have so many 'cribs' that students need do very little personal thinking, yet may appear to have a deep and detailed knowledge of the texts studied: education reduced to second-hand information rather than analytical tools.

Science: One of the most contentious topics in today's science curriculum is climate change. Science is a subject inextricably bound up with evidence and the interpretation of evidence. The overwhelming evidence at present supports the notion that the world is getting warmer. However, even this basic assertion must be seen in the light of long-term trends; and some of the evidence points to almost the opposite in the longer term. However, if we accept global warming as a given for the moment, then the real science has to be to search for reasons, and thus – ultimately – remedial actions. At this point the science becomes more contentious: for example, can we genuinely assess to what extent human actions are to blame or what the balance of natural phenomena is in the warming process? So recent news reports about Greta Thunberg and her activities raise ethical issues: Is the world really in an almost irreversible crisis? Is the alleged scientific evidence correct or mis-guided? Is there actually any need to panic at all? How much of the blame rests not with the actions of 'now' but with the misdeeds of the past (Hiroshima? World Wars?)? What blame rests with whom? Where do we go from here? Science is about the calm assessment of the best understandings and investigations we can get about an issue – in that context, how helpful is emotion and exploitation of people's fear? So, this 'objective' subject is, in truth, riddled with massive, and massively contentious, considerations.

WHY GOOD ETHICAL PRINCIPLES OFTEN FAIL

Lawrence Stenhouse wanted to make curriculum more honest (i.e. ethical); that is, he wanted to get teachers and children together dealing with topics 'in the round', not being rehearsed in information which may or may not be fully or partially true. HCP failed to catch on in more than a modest way for several reasons, educational and circumstantial. Espousing this philosophy of knowledge was a step too far for many educators; teaching through discussion and exploration is a methodology which requires advanced level teaching skills; gathering suitable resources takes time, energy and inventiveness; the government wanted simpler and controllable solutions (ostensibly to 'measure' the 'effectiveness' of schools and thus make them 'accountable'); the funding came to an end; so Lawrence's team split up and most acquired roles in which the research process became more important than the teaching elements of the work; and Lawrence himself, regrettably, died in his prime.

But the Three Pillars of Wisdom, as I think of them, are still worthy of consideration because they take us to the heart of how to compile and deliver a curriculum which has genuine value rather than one which can add up to a few assessed badges of achievement. Mischievously, I sometimes think that if people were awarded sleeve badges for GCSE and General Certificate of Education (GCE) successes, we would rapidly see the system for what it is: the Scouting movement of the educational world. Then we would get this kind of assessment-based learning into perspective.

CURRICULUM BUILDING: SOME PRINCIPLES

Curriculum building should, in my view, arise out of the world's two genuinely great questions. Though a visiting Martian might conclude otherwise, these are not: How many GCSEs/GCEs did you get? Will you get your first choice university through Clearing? They are, rather, these:

- Why?
- What is truth?

To me, these two questions, applied to curriculum building, try to explore first, what is worthy of inclusion in the curriculum (be that the formal learned material, or the 'hidden curriculum' conveyed through ethos etc.); and second, what are the most appropriate teaching methodologies through which to deliver those ideas?

The WHY of curriculum asks about the criteria for inclusion; and this is a question which must be answered on the macro level (the school's overall overt and hidden curriculum), the median level (the curricula of individual subject areas), and the micro level (what goes into this lesson?). At the macro level, I regard the Scottish Government's Document [13] *Curriculum for Excellence* (2008) as heading in the right direction when it identifies the following ambition for the curriculum as a whole:

- Opportunities to develop skills for learning, skills for life and skills for work for all young people at every stage.

Such an ambition in turn leads in the Document to these intentions, the order of which I have adapted to be more logical:

- A coherent and inclusive curriculum from 3 to 18 wherever learning is taking place, whether in schools, colleges or other settings
- A broad general education
- A focus on literacy, numeracy and health and wellbeing at every stage
- Appropriate pace and challenge for every child
- Ensuring connections between all aspects of learning and support for learning
- Time to take qualifications in ways best suited to the young person
- A focus on outcomes.

Learning skills, life skills and work skills – surely an unbeatable combination through which to guide the education of young people throughout school/college (3–18 years). What we are really looking at here is the obligation of the State to educate its citizens, and to do this so that they live both socially useful and personally fulfilling lives. That obligation could be summarised in the old proverb: To make people healthy, wealthy and wise. Interestingly, this notion was taken up as recently as 2017 as one of the mantras of the think-tank *The Learning and Work Institute*, which is concerned with lifelong education [14]. It is probably worth de-constructing the saying briefly lest anyone think it is jejune.

A curriculum for health: It was mainly down to the great social pioneers of the 19th Century to identify the links between educational failure and social disadvantage. Beginning with movements like the National Schools (which promoted education, especially literacy, among the poor), and to individual pioneers like Joseph Rowntree, Robert Owen and Charles Booth, the 19th and 20th centuries established beyond doubt that there were substantial links between lack of education on the one hand and social issues on the other. These movements established the negative effects of slum dwelling, malnourishment, polluted environments, parental alcoholism, family breakdown and child employment on children's education and general well-being. The message was: children from poor environments learn less well than other students.

There have been continuing studies from time to time through the modern eras which have confirmed beyond doubt this general picture about the links between poor social conditions and educational failure; but they have added some subtleties to the understanding, too. Typical was the longitudinal *Child Health and Education Study* [15] but there are numerous examples over the decades. The place of women in society in the pre-suffragette age depressed the education of girls – and this gender issue still manifests itself even if the circumstances of it change. Traditions within families of generational unemployment or low-grade working engender poor aspirations in children. Impoverishment does not relate solely to financial considerations: intellectual impoverishment (a lack of books, educational stimuli, even parental warmth) have their effects on children and their attitudes to learning. The growing trend for family break-up (which is now being felt even in traditional societies like that of Roman Catholic Malta) is a cause of trauma to youngsters. Mental health in the family, physical health of parents or children, the pressure for school-age children to be carers and so on, all impinge negatively on the potential for education to have its desired effect. To educate children, first one has to get the social conditions right.

Health in society, then, is not just medical and physical health – though it is that as well. Much had been done to improve children's physical health: from great discoveries such as penicillin, through pioneers of medical care from Florence Nightingale onwards, to the development of numerous preventative vaccines and immunisations – all of these have benefitted education directly and indirectly. But new problems emerge as society changes. Today's big issue is obesity (and its resultant diseases such as diabetes), borne on the back of a diminution of home-based meal preparation, cheap fast food, and over-indulgence which comes out of poor nutritional understandings.

What does all this add up to for curriculum building? However good a curriculum is, it cannot be entirely effective unless some conditions are met. The recipients of the curriculum (young people) must be physically and mentally fit to learn. The curriculum itself may be used to help the young people understand the need for fitness and mental health and how to achieve these. Aspects of society which act as barriers to children learning (for example, when a youngster has to act as a carer to an adult family member) have to be dealt with not by schools, but by politicians and social policy. Clearly, not all these social problems can be solved in schools, and schools should not be made either scapegoats for government failures or the means of putting them right when other, more radical, solutions are needed. Governments must identify and put right matters like poverty — schools deal with the Government's failures or partial successes. To this end, schools have established breakfast clubs, after-school clubs, or opened their doors very early in the morning to keep students off the streets and gainfully occupied. These activities often embody the hidden curriculum of health and well-being.

Within the school day, in the formal curriculum, schools need to take on board the educational implications: what to teach to produce citizens who — for example — understand nutrition, food preparation, canny shopping, personal hygiene, exercise, budgeting, saving, sound personal values, discernment (to help students avoid the blandishments of advertisers etc.), personal relations, and the many other factors which are implicit in what has been argued.

One of the great mysteries in the world of education is this: educators, researchers, political reformers, politicians and others have known beyond any doubt whatsoever that the negative links between the failures of social policy and the effectiveness of the educational process are real and chronic. Yet time and time again, Governments have failed to address these issues, and have even appeared, in varying degrees, to promote philosophies entirely counter to these basic needs of society. In our own time — right now — we can cite numerous examples; but let us content ourselves with just two. There can be no doubt that the gap between rich and poor has not closed, it has widened in recent decades — yet Governments, arguably, exacerbate the situation with revenue laws which favour the rich over against the poor: this, in turn, removes incentive and feeds young people with aspirations which eschew hard work and ambition, and favour instant fame and riches based on (for most) unlikely media success. This first point leads to a second: Who are the people in society most seen to be cultivated by politicians? Celebs: the minority superrich who can offer ostentatious but free hospitality and are rewarded by public acclamation of various kinds. In the end it comes down to where one puts one's values – which is another way of saying 'ethics'.

A curriculum for wealth: The State needs a healthy economy, and its citizens need a sufficient lifestyle. These two factors should help guide the school curriculum. At the individual level, students can reasonably expect that what they learn will put them on the road to suitable employment – an appropriate level of literacy and numeracy will underpin this, but also the basic understandings locked up in other subject areas, too. Wealth is not merely material wealth, but a fulfilment of personal life. So under this umbrella one can include a range of educational experiences spanning issues as diverse as general knowledge (not to be confused with intelligence), traditional culture, aesthetic activity, literature (as opposed to literacy), aspects of popular culture, technical skills, scientific understanding and so on. At a later stage in their education – at some time beyond the age of 16 or 18 – specific vocational or academic training might augment this process; but the roots of it should be there from the beginning. This element of the curriculum would include appropriate work-related skills such as timekeeping, punctuality, consistency, self-presentation; and more specific skills such as interview skills.

None of this education will happen unless the State has a coherent view of what it wants for itself and for its citizens. Many would argue that over recent decades we have seen a move away from the ideals of invention, design, manufacture, production and commerce; these have increasingly been replaced, it is claimed, by the 'knowledge economy' – i.e. the ability to sell expertise rather than goods. There are flaws in this: once the knowledge is imparted the knowledgeable may become redundant; and for those unable to participate, all that is left is the service sector characterised by low pay and low esteem.

This picture is simplified, and while bearing the hallmarks of truth may not be as clear-cut as it has been painted. Nevertheless, the educator needs to be aware of the ethics of a State moving its citizens towards goals which disadvantage some of them; an ethical curriculum demands that the very best chances are given to as many as possible. The shape of the curriculum we operate will tell us, and future generations, about our values.

A curriculum for wisdom: Wisdom implies two separate stages: the first is the acquisition of knowledge; the second is the ability to dwell and reflect on that knowledge to produce sound judgement. In this section I will dwell on knowledge acquisition; the more reflective process is dealt with elsewhere in the chapter and throughout the book. Knowledge acquisition is a controversial area: What should be taught? Each subject specialist has his/her own ideas and, of course, vested interests. So the approach which follows is not to lay down guidelines or even principles, but to ask you questions or make provocative statements which will have an ethical dimension to them. They are hard matters to face – but don't take umbrage, take thought!

MAKING CURRICULUM MORE ETHICAL

What follows asks you to complete the ACTION in order to start you thinking about some real curriculum issues which emanate from school subjects.

> **Action**
>
> Look at each of the curriculum areas which are listed below, whether you teach the subject area or not. In each case, react to the statements made about it. How can the curriculum of each of these subject areas be made more ethical in its content and in the way it is presented?

Mathematics

Given that this is the area with which most students struggle, should the maths curriculum not be examined more carefully to identify the most critical elements (elements for all); the things that relate to vocational activity of a non-specialist kind (which a large number of students might follow); and elements which suggest later specialisation (for a minority of students). Once this analysis is made, ought not the majority of students be freed from superfluous mathematical learning? Isn't this ethically fairer in that it would remove stress for many, avoid time wasting in schools?

Accepting that mathematics is considered a difficult area for many, shouldn't more effort be made in presenting it to explain maths topics a) through identifying the practical value of each item studied and b) how each might relate to life skills? In a nutshell – make relevance a guiding principle, perhaps? Learning for its own sake is a fine ideal, but in context isn't it ethically questionable to present material in a way that is merely theoretical?

Literacy

As with mathematics, literacy teaching must centre on skills which students can see and believe have practical application and purpose. Literacy is strongly functional in contexts as widely separate as making personal/social relations and becoming an employee in a major company. Ethically, no student should leave school without a strong functional skill in literacy, e.g. not being a reasonably fluent reader, not being able to express themselves clearly: these are major survival skills. Literacy skill should not just be an entitlement but also an absolute requirement of schools. So, what steps can schools take to ensure that this is the case?

Science

An old-fashioned view of science was that it was entirely 'objective', 'fact-based' and detached in its judgements. This is, of course, a fallacy, though its methodology should aim to be all of these things. The content of science is by no means as detached as some would have us believe. The following are typical of ethical questions which might arise out of the primary or secondary subject curriculum:

- To what extent must we consider the habitat needs of wild creatures given that human societies have needs which also need to be met? Is the crested newt colony more important than a new housing estate? What are the criteria for judgement?
- Should we impose vaccination/immunisation (which may not be entirely without risk) on young people or children to protect them and society at large from disease?
- In physics, some theories are just that, i.e. not facts. To adopt them may require something not so very far from what in religion might be counted as faith. Is this justifiable?

Religion

In a time when only a small minority practise the Christian religion, and a minority of the population of the UK claim any faith allegiance, is it justifiable (except in designated faith schools) to have a curriculum slot on the timetable with this label? Might not some more ethical approach be to restrict this element to, e.g., facts about faiths, the non-faith alternative and spiritual nourishment?

If there is conventional teaching about an individual faith, how does a teacher ensure that it is presented so that the students understand both what is claimed for it, and its legacy in the historical/modern worlds? Are the beliefs of non-believers fairly represented?

Religion as a genre is credited with much which is good and noble in the world; to what extent is this balanced by what is negative about it?

History

Much is claimed for the reliability of historical 'facts' – and doubtless this can be justified when these are about attested events such as dates. However, almost all history is taught through narrative, and those narratives are potentially subject to bias. How can the students distinguish between what is fact and what is interpretation?

Do historical resources in schools represent a genuine balance in dealing with the big issues of the subject – like Slavery, or Empire? How can the neutrality of the material used and the teacher's exposition be guaranteed? Is it clear, in the history lessons that, e.g., slavery has a long history in the story of nations and was perpetrated by many nations? In terms of Britain, does the teaching face the uncomfortable facts – like the involvement of Quakers in the British slave trade?

How justifiable is the 'testing' of history as it is now construed? Given that so much of the material is coloured by the perspectives of the tellers, would it not be more ethical to abandon testing altogether? Or to make history in schools far more evidence based than it is at present?

Geography

Geography as a subject discipline suffers from the same kinds of issues as do Religion and History. Geographers have to decide, for example:

- How do we represent the peoples whom the subject studies?
- What moral issues arise in studying countries and people? E.g. in studying the rain forest, how are the tensions between, and views of, the various interested parties (both within and outside the country concerned) represented in how the story is presented?
- What does geography have to say about the world distribution of resources, or about relative pollution from country to another, or about the rights of indigenous peoples past and present?

The visual and performing arts and physical education

These subject areas often require close contact for demonstration purposes and thus raise issues of a social nature:

- What means can teachers use to convey the subject skills without infringing personal space?
- In areas like art or photography, students sometimes ape society and produce images which have controversial content. How might this issue be dealt with when it arises? Has Political Correctness destroyed our ability to have an open dialogue about such issues?
- Many of these subject areas deal with concepts (both positive and negative) which reflect society – they deal on the one hand with 'beauty' and 'the good', and on the other with exposing evil and treating prejudice. How does a teacher steer a path through these issues?

Media and IT

The issues raised in the area of performing arts are all replicated in media studies, and in the use of IT. Other matters to be aware of might be:

- How might one deal with the thorny issue of the popular view that the camera never lies with the reality that every picture is edited from the moment the photographer frames the shot?
- To what extent can a teacher raise student awareness of the subtle differences which semantics can make in presenting a story?

Technologies

Technologies have a major part to play in modern life. At one end of the spectrum, the creative, they provide students with skills that have intrinsic value – what, after all, gives more satisfaction than a beautifully executed dovetail or clever piece of dyeing? But on the other hand, the practical, these skills provide excellent design (fitness for purpose) and may be altruistic (creating a more effective trolley for injured patients) – and they form the basis of much vocational training. But even design is not ethics-neutral, as Albrechtslund [16] correctly points out:

> ... the power of the designers to control the user is limited ... A theory of design ethics that does not distinguish between intentions and future practice might give users, legislators and others the impression that technology developed under certain guidelines are somehow certified 'foolproof' with regards to future ethical problems ....

This quotation hints at two issues which need to feature in this element of the curriculum: the use of well-intentioned creative technology for unintended, even unforeseen, unethical purposes; and the levels of blame this may place on the designer, however well intentioned.

Personal and social elements of curriculum

Personal and social education is perhaps the most obviously contentious of all in examining the ethics of curriculum. The issues are multiple, but a few examples suffice:

- Students may experience sex education classes, but these raise issues about the rights of parents to extract their children from them; the stigma that students may face if they don't participate; the nature of modern norms about sexuality and the conflicts these can produce for children from faith homes.
- Many schools make strong links with the police service; but I knew of one instance where a teacher flatly refused to take part because of an incident with the police in their own life which coloured their view indelibly. In these circumstances, dilemmas might be faced by the manager of this individual.

The hidden curriculum

The hidden curriculum refers, among other things, to the way in which the school wishes to put across attitudes, behaviour to other people, relations between student and student, relations between student and staff, students' behaviour outside school and so on.

A colleague of mine was closely associated with two outstanding schools, both with superb academic records, and both with enviable reputations for the ethos of the school and the way in which the students carried themselves in public at all times. Interestingly, he said, one was a faith school where all these matters were overtly linked to a religious conviction; the other (while fulfilling the law regarding such things as assemblies) was determinedly neutral on religion and followed a humanist-style code. My colleague noted that the outcomes in school atmosphere and pupil behaviour were so closely identical the institutions were interchangeable in every way. There may be many routes to ethical understanding: the outcome may be identical.

> **Action**
>
> Having considered these curriculum areas from an ethical perspective, have you discerned anything within them, and across the whole range, which has suggested that the kind of curriculum adopted might determine the kinds of teaching methods used? If so, what are your thoughts on this?

First thoughts on teaching an ethical curriculum

This chapter has now examined in some depth two of what I called Stenhouse's Pillars of Wisdom, philosophy and content, and we must consider briefly *Pillar 3: A suitable methodology for teaching*, i.e. how to communicate the curriculum which we have chosen. There are two points to make about this, but Stenhouse makes only one of them. My guess is this is because the other he regarded as so compellingly obvious.

The first point is that an open-ended curriculum like this needs open-ended methods to communicate it: for Stenhouse, this was primarily through discussion based on evidence – the latter provided through materials which could be extant or sought out specially. Class discussion played the absolutely central role as a means of learning, with the teacher acting as a 'neutral chairperson'. The 'voice' of this discussion was not about telling but about exploring together.

The second point is implicit in the first: such discussion and exploration depends on information which is not merely drawn from whatever subject forms the 'boundary' of the lesson (e.g. history, technology), but from any source. It is then, interdisciplinary. Evidence from any source is valid evidence in solving educational or intellectual problems.

These insights are the ones which will inform the next chapter, which is about ethical teaching methods for an ethical curriculum.

> **Action**
>
> For the moment, though, one is left with two queries to ponder: How can teachers, and teacher leaders, begin to take on board Pillars One and Two? At a deeper level, how can the teaching profession educate politicians and society into a deeper, more relevant, altogether wiser, view of curriculum?

This chapter and the next campaign for learning and teaching which are more exciting and useful. So, let me leave you with this contentious thought (anyone who has visited the millions of lodge-pole pines on the Canadian Rockies may empathise). Too much curriculum content is boring; students become like Annie Dillard's bear [17], who went exploring over the mountain but discovered the other side appeared precisely the same.

Covid-19 has had a more enduring effect on the work of schools than could have been envisaged, with most students learning from home. This has exacerbated some social problems highlighted in this book, and their ethical implications. But it has had the positive effect of encouraging lively debate among teachers about both curriculum and teaching methods. This could be a chance for significant change in schools when the epidemic is over.

5

ETHICAL PEDAGOGY

ETHICAL APPROACHES TO PEDAGOGY

Bertrand Russell [18] makes two critical points: that learning is about thinking, not about acquiring information *per se*; that it can only be communicated if students are treated in an adult way. Those brought up on Joyce Grenfell, look away now:

> When you want to teach children to think, you begin by treating them seriously when they are little, giving them responsibilities, talking to them candidly, providing privacy and solitude for them, and making them readers and thinkers of significant thoughts from the beginning. That's if you want to teach them to think.

In 1967, *The Observer* newspaper, realising that the only missing voices in debates about schooling were those of students, ran a competition which invited schoolchildren to write about 'the school that I'd like'. The results were edited into a book with the same title by Edward Blishen [19], a prolific author of texts for young people, and a former grammar-school boy (that is, not someone from, and conditioned by, the private education sector). I picked up a copy a couple of weeks ago, and found it oddly contemporary in its concerns, as well as full of insight and genuinely intelligent. It was slightly poignant in that the student writers were often wistful about the schooling they had wanted to enjoy and hadn't, yet the solutions were simple and affordable – they were mainly about attitudes to learning and teaching. Though the pages of my copy had browned with age and the cover was scuffed, the book was frequently very contemporary in its 'feel', which showed how little progress has been made beyond the superficial in the fifty years that had passed.

Bertrand Russell, in the quote above, has it just right: education is too frequently defined by learning things and not by **thinking about** things. Russell was a philosopher, but it is a view echoed by scientist Albert Einstein; and also by linguist Lev Vygotsky, who emphasised the need for talking by students so that they could learn to frame ideas.

It seems, then, that the only people who frequently fail to get this message are politicians and civil servants.

ETHICAL TEACHING METHODS CONSIDERED

If you cast your mind back to the chapter on the Ethical Curriculum, it was suggested that such a curriculum needed ethical teaching methods. They, in turn, would be predicated on investigation, evidence, discussion and open-endedness. Let's be clear: I am not saying that every instance and use of didactic teaching is wrong or unethical – if anyone credits me with that view, then that's their own distortion not mine. Periods of didactic teaching activity in the classroom can be (a) useful, (b) economic and (c) entertaining – while still being educational. Let's examine those three statements.

Didactic episodes are sometimes useful because they focus the attention of all the students on some aspect of their learning at the same time. Operationally and managerially this is helpful to students and teachers from time to time. Sometimes such episodes allow all the students to share the same knowledge simultaneously, even if this is a prelude to students moving off at tangents later; they are economic of everybody's time and energy. Didactic episodes can be educational yet simultaneously entertaining; for example, a good exposition of some historical event, or the reading of a poem, or sharing a newspaper report of a scientific discovery. But here, I shall put the argument for making the didactic episode just one tool in the teacher's armoury, and not the central weapon in it – certainly not the central weapon it has become due to pressure to cover the syllabus and coercion to answer examination questions – which last are sometimes themselves simply closed, not only in format but in thinking terms too.

The ethical curriculum which was described in the last chapter suggested that real education is not solely or even primarily about information but about the power to think – exactly the point supported by Russell, Einstein and Vygotsky. If this trio played cricket equally as well as they pursued their actual careers, they would form the strongest line-up of batsmen in world history at one, two and three – so maybe we ought to take them seriously.

Thinking does not come out of being told things, but out of having experiences, raising questions, trying to answer those queries, using evidence, weighing evidence, discussing the evidence with others, comparing and contrasting viewpoints, making connections, challenging, delving deeper into sources to clarify the outcomes of these deliberations. More of this gets done in primary school in the British system of education than it does in secondary schools – this is down to the pressure of examinations: secondary schools have always been exam-obsessed, and primaries have become more so in the light of SATs tests. It is at least arguable that schools and students have increased their capacity for fact-absorption and regurgitation significantly as a result; but have lost the many vital components of the educated person.

Interestingly, students seem to be more aware of this than teachers, and much more aware than politicians and civil servants. Back to Blishen's collection of young peoples' insights, and they make three absolutely critical points. First the negative, a view of how things were (and at the risk of offence, often still are):

> 'Now, do you all understand?' asks the frowning maths master impatiently. Silence. 'Right then, get on with pages 72–76.' The heads bow down and pens begin to scratch. A few poor boys, still not understanding, sit waiting anxiously for the bell. Others glance at the clock every few minutes. The bell goes and the tension breaks; everyone hurriedly packs his books and heaves a sigh of relief. The master walks out and the next walks in. Another forty tedious minutes…' (Stephen, 13)

Next, a mind-boggling exposition of true education by a young man of just seventeen:

> 'The roots of education are bitter, but the fruit is sweet,' wrote Aristotle; but need the roots be so unpalatable? When learning

ceases to be looked upon by the majority of schoolchildren as a chore, but instead as a sequence of processes just as enjoyable, and more fulfilling than their normal out-of-school activities, then our educational system will have justified itself. After all, education is <u>not</u> an entity in itself, wrapped up tightly and isolated in protective cloth. Schools must allow pupils to recognise them for what they are (or should be) – a means for gaining access to and absorbing all the exciting and stimulating things that are around them.

The school I would like to see would strive to cater not for artificial ends such as examinations (which are frequently tests of <u>what</u> one knows, not <u>how</u> this knowledge has been gained and to what advantage), but instead treat the artistic and scientific fulfilment of the largest number of pupils as an end in itself. (Kenneth, 17 – his emphasis)

And lastly, a young girl's important point about both teacher and student being on the same learning journey:

Lessons must be a mixture or combined effort by teacher, machine [at this date the students often use machine meaning computer – ed], and pupil. (Nina, 14)

Action

When did you last genuinely learn alongside your students? Some teachers do, but many never do: they rest on their status as professionals, dispensing information to others. How did you learn alongside them, e.g.

- Did you set them to write a poem and then write one alongside them and under the same constraints?
- Did you ask them to use IT to explore some new information, and do so alongside them and share your own findings?
- Did you ask them to make something, and make the same thing alongside them so they could see you doing it (including any errors)?

How fair would 'learning together' be as a description of your teaching style?
Did you baulk at this task because you think teachers shouldn't reveal their weaknesses?

HARD QUESTIONS ABOUT ETHICAL PEDAGOGY

In terms of ethics, what have we discovered to date about teaching methods? First, that education is not primarily about imparting information, but is about encouraging students to develop thinking skills, with all that these entail. Second, that reliance – certainly over-reliance – on didactic teaching fails to achieve this aim. There is an implicit goal in the teaching-learning process of making material engaging for the students. A sophisticated approach requires the realisation that the value of education is intrinsic: learning for learning's sake. We have also seen that teachers and students are both learners: this is not merely an expert/novice business. All of this implies that 'lessons' or learning sessions will be predicated on enquiry; they will be active, open and evidence-based. Guidance of these sessions is not the sole responsibility of the teacher. Ethically, what this series of insights does is to put at the forefront of education the yardstick that in its intention and its delivery the process and outcomes belong to the student: a perception with which the education 'system' repeatedly loses touch. At the level of the classroom it is the teacher's role to be aware of this ethical approach; but at the department or faculty level it is for the middle manager who leads others to assure him/herself that these approaches are in place.

The learning scenario just described does happen in schools: from time to time in many schools, and often in a smaller proportion of schools – but it does not routinely happen (especially in secondary schools). It is not the norm of educational provision. If we seek reasons for why this is the case, then answers boil down to two: examination pressure and the fact that this kind of learning demands far more thought of the tutor than does compiling a few pre-existing resources and giving a presentation or even just using a textbook. The core skills of this kind of student-centred working are easy enough to identify, but in a book of this scope and purpose cannot be described at length. What follows is a short summary, along with some hints on where to find more detail.

QUESTIONING

Good lessons flow from teachers posing problems and issues to students and allowing them to explore their way towards answers.

These questions need to be open, and they need to be about learning. Questions can be sub-divided into types using a typology which goes back to Benjamin Bloom, but which has been resurrected by a number of scholars over time. Two of the practitioner implications for this kind of learning are that:

- Sessions might begin with or contain a mix of lower order questions and high order ones – the high order asking students to apply, analyse and evaluate things they have studied
- Students might benefit from reflecting on how they learn – i.e. the metacognitive process.

My own research in this field suggested that (at the time) too little of teachers' energy (less than 10%) went into high order activity – a crucial component of working in this way had to be to free the genuine 'thinking' from the welter of lower order tasks and the clutter of regurgitation that went on in classrooms. Recent, informal, observations have not persuaded me much has changed.

EXPLAINING

When parts of lessons are used to present material in the didactic mode, then the quality of the explanations offered should be of the highest order. It may not be overt, but usually explanations offer the answers to questions, though the questions themselves may not be obvious; e.g. what, how and why questions. Quality explanations usually exhibit a number of characteristics about their construction which make them effective in capturing the attention of the listener and sustaining their internal logic. These are encapsulated in Table 5.1 at the end of the chapter.

DIFFERENTIATING

Not all students work at the same pace or achieve the same standards: this is true even when classes are streamed or setted. Many teachers are satisfied with the relatively superficial notion that differentiation takes place of itself because students cover more or less ground in the allotted time-frame, achieve different levels in the task, or understand in more or less sophisticated ways compared with their peer group. But this is not the essence of true differentiation in teaching. The onus is on the teacher to prepare tasks for a given lesson, which will give different students different but appropriate levels at which to achieve; the teacher will provide extension tasks for those who work quickly and more demanding tasks for those who work at a higher cognitive level; there may even need to be special tasks for students with particular needs and who may (or may not) get support from a teaching assistant. It is the teacher's job to be on top of these needs and meet them.

USING METACOGNITION; AND THE SKILLS FOR INDEPENDENT LEARNING

One way to encourage students to learn more effectively is to use the metacognitive process, i.e. to get students to reflect on their own learning, and what learning and teaching methods work best for them as individuals. Students who reflect on their own means of learning, learn better. In the same way, students who have some control over decisions within learning – when to move to a new topic, how to explore it, how to express or record it, are more fulfilled in their learning. Self-marking is just one of the ways in which this might happen (but this does not relieve the teacher of their assessment role).

HAVING APPROPRIATE CLASS MANAGEMENT SKILLS TO MAKE PARTICIPATORY LESSONS HAPPEN

Since it has been suggested that the education of these students will be more student-centred, participatory, open-ended and investigative, there can be no room for time to be wasted on class management and control. The up-side of this observation is that students are likely to be very much more engaged in lessons and therefore very much less likely to behave poorly because of boredom and poor teacher delivery. Class management has been discussed, too, in a previous chapter.

What ethical criteria, then, do lessons of this ilk, using these teaching skills and approaches, meet? Four such criteria might be:

Engagement: The approach advocated here is designed to maximise students' time-on-task, and the levels of effectiveness at which they work in line with their individual capabilities. Effective engagement with learning is a fundamental principle of schooling, and an obligation on schools and their staff.

Valuing ideas: In the process of effectiveness of engagement and achievement sight has not been lost – indeed, has been in-built – of the importance of making all learning student-centred and interesting: to inculcate and model a desire to learn.

Respect and equality: Students' individuality and the individual needs, are respected by the actions described.

Detachment: By using the methods described, any bias on the part of the teacher (to which students are exposed for an inordinate amount of time) is lessened, and thus a greater objectivity is given to learning.

> **Action**
>
> Leaders need, of course, to be aware of the kind of learning and teaching which is happening within their areas of responsibility. Together with your staff members, undertake an inventory of how your curriculum is taught to each year group. Would it pass the kinds of scrutiny identified above as denoting ethical learning/teaching? If there are gaps in the provision, plan to put them right.

These outcomes are all items which meet ethical demands for the education of young people to operate effectively, enjoyably and to the highest standards. But there may, of course, be objections. I have contrasted this kind of learning with cramming for public examinations. There **may** be a case to be made within our society as it stands for examination passes in schools to be maximised as a way of increasing students' life-chances; students and their parents expect this last of schools. But let's not lose sight of the fact that during the 2020 Covid-19 outbreak, when examinations proved too risky, systems were put in place, with very little disruption, to assess students' suitability for Higher Education; examinations were suddenly no longer the imperative they had been the previous year! So how does the middle leader or the classroom teacher square the circle on this? [Author's note: At the time of writing this statement was correct. Shortly afterwards the Government and Ofqual stepped in, and chaos broke out.]

THE STUDENT ROLE IN ETHICAL PEDAGOGY

Some teachers believe passionately that their 'expertise' in a subject is what counts most in the education of the student; and it is true that being passionate is important in learning. So how can this be harnessed within the kind of ethical teaching put forward above?

Some teachers believe, equally passionately, that students are not capable of making decisions about their own education. Though conducted in the context of learning citizenship skills, the Report *Inspiring Schools: a Literature Review* [20] concluded as follows:

Research indicates that students who have the opportunity to choose school activities show enhanced motivation. The component elements of self-determination include (but are not limited to):

- Choice making
- Decision making
- Problem solving
- Goal setting and attainment
- Independence, risk taking and safety
- Self-observation, evaluation and reinforcement
- Self-instruction
- Self-advocacy and leadership
- Internal locus of control
- Positive attributions of efficacy and outcome
- Expectancy
- Self-awareness
- Self-knowledge.

The issue of students' involvement in **how** they learn (and the argument extends to **what** they learn) is an interesting one. Traditionally, the theory of teaching applied to adults was known as androgogy; and that applied to younger students was pedagogy. Pedagogy had a greater degree of imposition implicit in the process because it was deemed that students could not (or should not) make (or participate in) these decisions. Hence the word pedagogue is used to describe a strict or pedantic teacher, or anyone who is always pontificating: teacher knows best. (You know the old joke about teachers on holiday abroad: you can always pick them out in the hotel dining room because they talk louder, more often, and more opinionatedly than anyone else.) However, a more modern notion is that of heutagogy, which implies a degree of control on the part of the learner over what is learned, how it is learned, and when it is learned (i.e. to match with the need to know or their current interests). All theories or systems have the built-in danger of too rigid application; but there is a real need in our current, tightly controlled education system, to hand back some initiative to learners – which is what the *Inspiring Schools* report tries to do.

Ethical questions, in life and education, are never simple; but we do have to weigh the options and come to rational conclusions based on ultimate good (as far as we can define it) in the contexts in which we find ourselves.

Action

As leader, ask your staff to have an in-depth debate on the ways in which it is possible to satisfy both what we have called the ethical curriculum and the demands of the examination curriculum. Produce a set of guidelines for everyone to follow.

INTERDISCIPLINARY LEARNING AND TEACHING: A KEY TO ETHICAL PEDAGOGY

One of the two key ethical approaches to teaching methods lies, it has been argued so far, in presenting material in such a way that the learning process produces independent learning and higher order thinking skills in students – and that means using investigative techniques, experiential learning, and critical approaches to evidence. The second key approach flows from this view and it is this: learning should, wherever possible, take place in an interdisciplinary context. Martha Boles [21] captures the essence like this:

> This world is of a single piece; yet, we invent nets to trap it for our inspection. Then we mistake our nets for the reality of the piece. In these nets we catch the fishes of the intellect but the sea of wholeness forever eludes our grasp. So, we forget our original intent and then mistake the nets for the sea.

I argued the case for interdisciplinary approaches at length in my 2011 volume *Cross-curricular Teaching in the Primary School,* but I expanded and extended the argument to both primary and secondary schools in the 2015 second edition (Chapters 1 and 2). For this reason, I am not going to rehearse the whole justification here though I am going to provide a précis of it in what follows [22]. To preface that, I am also going to make a couple of bold claims. First, that the argument put forward in the 2015 text is sufficiently detailed as to be compelling; second, that it is irrefutable by any fair-minded person.

However, you need to challenge me at this point with a question: 'Why is an interdisciplinary approach more ethical than one based on self-contained elements of knowledge? (Call these subjects or any other label you choose.) In a nutshell the answer is this: because, obtaining the most detailed and rounded view of a problem or an issue is the nearest we can get to the truth of it – and an ethical approach to knowledge has to seek the most reliable picture possible. We owe that to our students.

The supposed reality of subject disciplines is, in fact, a half-truth. As Boles's quotation suggests, we label elements of knowledge for convenience; the labels are sometimes useful but do not define or confine knowledge. In the real, grown-up, post-school world it is the interdisciplinary approach that solves real-world problems.

By thinking in subject-bound ways, we restrict ourselves and others. Ironically, one of the best examples is the subject labelled physics. At the level of simple electric circuits or gravity it might be argued that physics has its own 'discipline', i.e. way of thinking and working which is unique to it (the nature of so-called 'disciplines' is at the heart of the adherence to the subject view of knowledge). But move onto the higher levels, and it becomes indistinguishable from other forms of knowledge. For example, theoretical physics is often about things we can't easily demonstrate or even see, in which it is necessary to believe in order to produce a tentative theory of how the world works. This stands closer to theology, perhaps, than it does to any other academic discipline – it requires 'faith' even if that faith is subsequently disproved (by experimentation) and replaced by a new 'revelation' (scientific law). So why compartmentalise knowledge under subject labels to begin with? In fact, let's return to the source of our first quotation in this section, Boles; she goes on to say:

> Three of these nets we have named Nature, Mathematics and Art. We conclude they are different because we call them by different names. Thus, they are apt to remain forever separated with nothing bonding them together. It is not the nets that are at fault but rather our misunderstanding of their function as nets. They do catch the fishes but never the sea, and it is the sea that we ultimately desire.

If you want to see a synthesis of nature, good scientific knowledge and observation, and superb literary skills working together, look no further than the poem *Owl* by George Mann MacBeth (you can google this: https://www.fromtroublesofthisworld.wordpress.com/2015/12/27/0wl-by-george-macbeth).

So why is there such resistance in English education to interdisciplinary approaches? Most teachers tend to define themselves by what they perceive as their 'expertise' ('I'm a geographer/historian/linguist) or the age group in which they specialise; they even conduct social introductions in the same vein! What is suggested here is different: that such, much vaunted, 'expertise' is actually a limitation. *Education Scotland* [23] produced an interesting set of assertions which I have paraphrased:

> Learning beyond subject boundaries provides learners with the opportunity to experience deep, challenging and relevant learning. It rehearses some important advantages for teachers, too: this approach makes clear connections between and across curriculum areas; it makes planning more logical and involves the learners in active, collaborative learning, with challenging and thought-provoking tasks, which lead to critical thinking. It provides the learner with a more coherent experience; it improves assessment by involving the learner in discussion of their knowledge.

Let it be clear at this point: interdisciplinary approaches to learning and understanding do not reject disciplines; they embrace them, subsume them, break down barriers between them, link them, apply them, improve their relevance and augment them. By linking areas of human knowledge (subjects, if you must), interdisciplinary thinking is inevitably higher order thinking – the learner cannot avoid analysing and making connections, synthesizing the links and making new and over-arching sense of the problem or subject matter. Not the sour milk, then, (as some portray it) of educational practice – but the crème de la crème.

But maybe you are not quite convinced yet: You think that 'subjects' can somehow have a wholly independent and absolutely isolationist existence? Another example, then – this time from the so-called discipline of history.

Historians ask two sets of questions about their 'discipline' (*historians* ask them, so they must be the right questions). The first is about historicity; the second about historiography. Very baldly, historicity explores the historical actuality of people or happenings, meaning that there is demonstrable evidence of them as opposed to their being an historical myth, legend or fiction. Historicity means we consider the statement factual. OK – so that deals with the nuts and bolts: we can sometimes be fairly secure – e.g. the Battle of Hastings was genuinely fought in 1066. But, unfortunately, most history comes in the form of text – most history is historiography, i.e. writing of, or about, events of the past. Now de-constructing that transports us – willy-nilly – into an interdisciplinary world that throws open the Pandora's history box of the universe!

It's tempting to take an uncritical view of historical writing, i.e. to accept that the narrative is (largely) true. But take Caesar's *Gallic Wars*; while some of the content may have happened, the book was a piece of blatant self-promotion. Clearly, then there is an issue about sorting out some basics: what really happened, what was alleged to have happened but didn't or was distorted, what was left out (judicious editing is prevalent in all walks of life), what was 'sexed up' to magnify Caesar – and so on. And if you think this only happens in ancient history (i.e. history written a long time ago), dream on, as the song says. So immediately we are into issues of truth – and ethics. Historiography is about for sorting the facts from the layers of interpretation.

Since most history is written – whether it be ancient or modern – it has to be viewed against the criteria of literary criticism. Historical narrative may be constructed against the criteria of its time: social mores; norms of society; current philosophies such as Marxism. We might say: 'History is not so much fact as literary artefact'. If we want to get technical, post-modernists and de-constructivist historians suggest that written history consists of 'plot' which is invented as much as discovered by historians. It employs four tropes: metaphor, metonymy, synecdoche and irony. Foucault, the French philosopher, claims that all history is ideologically contaminated; there is no objective certainty about historical writing — in other words it does not represent 'truth' in any absolute sense of the word. (To return to an earlier point, that's a good reason for rejecting the 'dates and facts' school of examining history.)

Let us see these points in action. A Guardian article by David Olusoga (12.07.15) [24], a respected academic, rales solidly against the British involvement in the slave trade. You can read this article for yourself on-line to confirm that the summary of key points made below is accurate:

- History books 'bury' the British part in slavery
- Many notable British families grew rich on the slave trade in the 17th and 18th centuries, but have erased those episodes from their history, often by semantics used in commemorating their relatives
- Often, these slave traders are written about as heroic characters
- William Wilberforce, widely celebrated as the great abolitionist, is also widely used as a shield to protect Britain from criticism from its role in slavery
- Implicitly, this has been a deliberate national amnesia.

Texts like Olusoga's might well be used in history lessons: his article is the work of a good academic, persuasively written and certainly contains truth. Teachers use these kinds of resource quite frequently; they are accessible and have some quality. But teachers do not often stop to ask about the deeper questions raised by this kind of de-contextualised use of materials. Olusoga is right: thousands of British families grew rich on this trade; the historic roles of some individuals have been airbrushed; arguably, Wilberforce might be popularly construed as a 'get out of jail' card. The trade was totally despicable for all the obvious reasons. It is obscene that people grew rich on it. Britain was, for a time, at the forefront of it. But ...

As it stands, it is not the **whole** story — which is why presenting material in this way **could** be construed as ethically questionable — not for what it says, but for what it omits. This is exactly the error of assuming the camera never lies while, in reality, every picture is edited in some way. Olusoga's historical vignette shows exactly why the 'discipline' of history does not have ultimate integrity as Truth or even as fact unless the partialness of the statements made is openly acknowledged. History, of this kind and all kinds, needs to be given an interdisciplinary context. Slavery was a not very elevating element in the British Empire; but the British Empire – however despicable in part – had its upsides too. It did contribute some real and lasting benefits. As for slaves, while for a time Britain cashed in on the wealth to be made through it, Britain did not invent slavery; the trade had been going on for centuries before the Transatlantic horrors perpetrated by Britain (though that in no way excuses Britain's participation). Olusoga certainly doesn't say it, but many writers present slavery only as a white vs black scenario; that is also not true; the origins of slavery seem to go back to the Middle East; it crosses cultures, nationalities and even religions; it crosses not just centuries but millennia. It becomes a habit of victorious armies of any race, creed, colour or religion; it is perpetrated by the powerful on both others and on their own people. In the past, it is shameful that people claiming to espouse Christian ethics and their churches (for example, the Quakers) contaminated themselves with the trade (though Quakers were also numbered among the abolitionists). Historically many slaves were white and Christian. In Franco's Spain in the 1930s, Spaniards enslaved Spaniards. The even more recent Nazi régime made slaves of tens of thousands, mostly white people. In today's Britain there have been small-scale but equally dastardly examples of rich individuals enslaving poor individuals – only some of the perpetrators were white or British. What comes out of this discussion is that students need to be given a range of perspectives; and the critical tools to use them. Otherwise they only repeat the prejudices of their forebears. To go a step further, they might also be encouraged to look down at their designer trainers, and ask where they came from, who made them, how much the workers were paid, what levels of freedom they enjoy, and who is responsible. The answers to all these issues are not clear-cut, not simple and certainly not instant. Had Stenhouse (see Chapter 4) been teaching this material he would have balanced the picture; and the quality of understanding and education that resulted would have risen exponentially.

There are two great ethical truths in this chapter: the first is that we need to take careful stock of how we present material to students so that we provide for them a learning experience that is engaging and interesting; but the material we present needs to take into account the whole story not our edited extracts from it. What teachers do, how they teach, how students learn, may be legal, may be the norm for our generation; yet they ought also to answer a higher question – are they ethical? But one has to recognise that this is dangerous ground: there are in society many powerful interests that would not welcome this degree of honesty nor the creation of a generation who could genuinely question, think and reason as opposed to adopting mantras and repeating them. No-one said ethics were easy.

I will draw this section of the argument to a close with another quote from 17-year-old Kenneth (in Blishen's book):

> I believe the first step necessary is to dilute or even destroy, rigid arbitrary divisions chopping up schooling into nicely compact subjects. This division is by its very nature artificial… This integration of subjects should be based primarily on the vast amount of experience potentially available from outside the rather restrictive walls of school.

DRAWING TOGETHER THE THREADS OF ETHICAL PEDAGOGY

This chapter has covered a lot of ground; so let us try to draw together the threads of the argument for ethical pedagogy as they have emerged to date. What does an ethical teacher try to do in lessons?

An ethical teacher:

- Develops a philosophy of education/teaching/learning. This text has suggested that an appropriate philosophy mirrors Russell's 'learning means thinking' and that education means learning how to interrogate material to establish the best truth possible (it rarely becomes Truth).
- Employs teaching methods that are designed to achieve this philosophy – varied methods of presentation, fitted to the purpose of each lesson episode: e.g. a didactic episode to share information or insight; an investigative episode to draw out students' creativity and reasoning. These methods are designed to maximise students' interest and encourage curiosity and a desire to explore, de-construct, reason and learn more.

- Manages the learning process so that it proceeds smoothly, and there is no unnecessary disruption, which might interfere with others' ability to learn, or degenerate into negative personal relationships or conflicts between students, even cause stress and poor mental health. Ethical pedagogy encourages everyone's contribution and flags up its value.
- Takes into account the different abilities of all students in the group, differentiating work for groups or individuals as appropriate so that they can benefit fully and contribute effectively.
- Encourages students to be self-determined in their learning rather than teacher dependent by giving them opportunities to make decisions and by encouraging students to use the techniques of metacognition to inform their awareness of how they learn.
- Learns alongside the students to communicate that learning is a 'forever' process.
- Encourages interdisciplinary understandings in order to promote the widest and deepest approach to knowledge and truth. This implies the removal of the teacher's own bias from controversial issues.

These insights reflect back the five principles we established in the previous chapter as ways of implementing the ethical curriculum:

- High quality and varied learning experiences
- Unbiased approaches
- Integrity in presentation
- Student participation in their own learning
- A degree of student control.

MAKING ETHICAL DECISIONS ABOUT PEDAGOGY

To date, we have examined some aspects of pedagogy, and whether or not these represent ethical behaviour for teachers in delivering best practice. But we need to glance, too, at the more generalised notion of how to make ethical decisions about pedagogy.

Though some people disagree, I would contend that there are no right or wrong answers whenever we consider ethical dilemmas – our answers are, almost by definition, bounded by variables: time, context, immediate circumstance, the nature of individuals concerned at that moment, changing external pressures – and bigger issues that apply to us such as policies, official directives, the law and so on. What we have to strive for is the best answer at the time and in the circumstance.

In deciding a course of action, these things seem to be recurrent and important about our thinking:

- Identifying the problem/s accurately and in detail
- Considering all potential options and alternatives
- Looking at possible consequences for those involved, e.g., learners: the possible good and the possible bad, in each course of action
- Weighing options to decide maximum benefit
- Avoiding personal bias or dogma in making a decision
- Making the best decision in good faith; explaining it; and implementing it consistently – and being willing to change or modify when new evidence comes to light.

To help you get the flavour of pedagogical dilemmas in practice I am going to end the chapter by asking you to argue the case for and against the same pedagogical issue.

Action

Thinking through grouping for learning and mixed ability teaching

Carry out both tasks to maximise your benefit from this ACTION.

1 As a teacher: In readiness for the new school year, you are asked to teach students in mixed ability groups using the kinds of methods we have discussed in this chapter. These mixed ability groups will replace the streamed classes you have been used to. You don't find the rationale for this very well formulated by the school; so you resolve – prior to undertaking any lesson preparation – to construct, with ethical issues in mind, your own rationale for the change of teaching approach. Make a list of the key points that your rationale would include, both for and against the change.

2 As a leader: In a school which has traditionally used mixed ability teaching methods and the teaching approaches suggested in this chapter, the SLT suddenly proposes to stream all classes in the new academic year. The declared intention is to improve results in national tests. You are asked for your department's reaction to this proposed change, and to submit a short (one side of A4) paper summarising your view and the reasons for it. Draft the paper with an eye on the ethical principles involved, as you see them.

SUMMARY

Because this chapter has dealt with a very wide-ranging topic, it has had to be selective in the aspects covered. However, in the next chapter, three specific teacher activities are examined in a little more detail: lesson planning, assessment, and homework.

Table 5.1 Components of an effective explanation

Create a dynamic introduction	Capture attention and create interest
Define all key terms or concepts	Otherwise the explanation won't make sense
Link the explanation with concrete experience	Students learn best through tangible experience
Use positive and negative examples	Both can be useful
Build in tasks	Link the talk with doing
Introduce and use technical language	To expand the students' conceptual understanding
Develop rules and principles	These are part of higher order thinking
Use connectives to enhance meaning	Appropriate use of language is important
Exploit linguistic ploys	Things like: 'this is important' or 'listen carefully now'
Use repetition and emphasis	Use your voice and intonation as well as just words
Adopt an appropriate pace	Important, to keep everyone on-side
Number points if necessary	This helps to structure your thinking and theirs
Use humour	Everyone remembers better when things are light-hearted
Link the explanation to existing knowledge	Show where new knowledge links with old
Build in the feedback loop	Find ways (often questions) to check understanding at critical points

Source: From Kerry, T. *Explaining and Questioning* (2002) Nelson Thornes.

6

ETHICAL LESSON PLANNING, ASSESSMENT AND HOMEWORK

ETHICAL LESSON PLANNING

To deliver an ethical curriculum using ethical methods of pedagogy pre-supposes ethical lesson planning. If you were to ask me what the difference is between lesson planning and ethical lesson planning, I would say, in a word, 'intention'.

There are a myriad ways in which to plan lessons, and plenty of examples of proformas which can be used to help in that process. Each has its merits, and you might choose a favoured one which fits your context. There is an example at the end of the chapter in Table 6.1, but it is not in any sense a model to be followed uncritically; not every lesson should be planned in exactly the same way. But lesson plans will have common features, which will include these:

- A title for the lesson (to keep your thinking focused)
- The intentions for the lesson (i.e. what do you hope to achieve?)
- Awareness of where the lesson fits into a sequence
- Lesson content (the key ground to be covered)
- Learning and teaching method(s) (any explanation to be given; key questions to be asked; use of discussion; use of evidence, etc.)
- Resources needed (key item (s), plus others in anticipation of where the lesson might lead; and necessary equipment)
- Tasks to be set (not every lesson will have a major task associated with it, but some will)
- Differentiation of tasks (how the intention of the task or its instructions can be adapted to keep, e.g., the brightest, the fast but superficial workers, the slowest, etc., working on the task and achieving something worthwhile)

- Assessment (if there is any, an explanation to students of what is expected, at what level and how the assessment will operate – e.g. teacher marking, self-marking, peer marking)
- Plenary and feedback (how the lesson might end by drawing the learning together, sharing insights, reflecting on how the learning took place, i.e. metacognition, and, probably, a thought or question for students to go away and ponder before next time)

So where does intention come in and why is it different when lessons are planned with an eye to their ethical value? It works something like this:

Hundreds of thousands of lessons are planned every day up and down the country. Many plans will have a line or two under a heading which might be 'aims and intentions for the lesson'. For my part, I tend to avoid 'aims' because aims are longer-term than a single lesson – they belong more appropriately to a unit of work or a term's experience. Objectives are more immediate, but my preference is for intentions – things which the teacher wants the students to be able to do today; and they are divisible into the new knowledge, newly acquired skills and fresh understandings which the teacher hopes to draw out from the class. It is at this point that 'intention' in an ethical sense comes into its own.

Too many lessons have intentions to impart new knowledge or even skills (teaching) without new understanding (learning) as we saw in the discussion of Ofsted in Chapter 4. In that case, though it isn't spelled out, the true intention is back to that hoary old pair of chestnuts: getting through the syllabus and passing the test, whatever it may be. So what makes the intentions for a lesson – and the lesson itself – ethical is the recognition that this lesson (every lesson) needs to help to change, mould, inform or modify the students' understanding – lessons are about learning – that is, Bertrand Russell's view that learning equals thinking, and not (merely) about teaching the prescribed content. Thinking can be **about** content, but it should **never be ousted by** content:

> Our great mistake in education is, as it seems to me, the worship of book-learning – the confusion of instruction and education. We strain the memory instead of cultivating the mind. The children in our elementary schools are wearied by the mechanical act of

writing, and the interminable intricacies of spelling; they are oppressed by columns of dates, by lists of kings and places, which convey no definite idea to their minds, and have no near relation to their daily wants and occupations… We ought to follow exactly the opposite course with children–to give them a wholesome variety of mental food, and endeavour to cultivate their tastes, rather than to fill their minds with dry facts. The important thing is not so much that every child should be taught, as that every child should be given the wish to learn. What does it matter if the pupil knows a little more or a little less? A boy who leaves school knowing much, but hating… lessons, will soon have forgotten almost all he ever learned; while another who had acquired a thirst for knowledge, even if he had learned little, would soon teach himself more than the first ever knew. (John Lubbock d. 1913) [25]

Lubbock's view is still valid and necessary – and, avoiding the cliché of the time, applies equally to females as males – today as then: the terrifying thing is not that his prose looks to us a touch anachronistic, but that it still needs to be said a century on.

Having reviewed, in Chapters 4 and 5, ethical approaches to curriculum and to learning, it was necessary to note briefly in this chapter how what we discovered previously needs to be applied to the planning process and put into action: that the central concerns are about skills like understanding, discernment and judgement, not about information. But you have grasped the point by now and the issue does not need to be laboured here; you can follow the gist in practical terms in the Table at the end of the chapter, which adds the ethical dimension to a lesson plan. So now, the time has come to take a look at the later end of the process – during- or post-lesson assessment; but first, carry out the ACTION below.

Action

If you are a middle leader, part of whose role is to look at lesson plans, how do you take into account those factors which make the content and learning ethical? How do you persuade staff to be more aware of these factors when they are planning? If you are a teacher, how do you build an ethical dimension into your lesson plans?

ETHICAL APPROACHES TO ASSESSMENT

There are really three major kinds of assessment – feedback; marking of students' work; and formal testing/assessment.

Feedback is a continuous process: the whole time that a teacher is engaging with students – talking, questioning, circulating to check on books, listening – he/she is making judgements about students' understanding and picking up clues as to how to proceed with further learning.

Marking is typically the teacher responding to a classroom task. So maybe the teacher has asked the student/s to write a review of the main causes of King Harold being defeated at the Battle of Hastings. The teacher will then look over the student/s' written responses to see whether they are correct or how insightful they are about the relative importance of the items listed.

Assessment, as a label, is reserved here for a formal processing of examination: SATs, GCSE, GCE or mock tests; and any similar formal tests which schools choose to make – such as end-of-year exams.

Any form of judgement about student performance should share certain characteristics in order to be ethical: it should be fair and accurate and should also provide guidance for improvement. However, the descriptors here are themselves open to debate. What is fair, and fair to whom? How accurate can marking, for example, ever be?

Let's take two quick examples which could have been set to the same students in the same class. Task 1 runs: If Hadrian had not built his Wall across Northumberland, where might he have built instead, and why? Task 2 says: Plot on a map the line of Hadrian's Wall. It is clear Task 1 requires a lot more, and higher order, thinking than Task 2. So, one variable in the value of the learning is not down to the students' answers but the teacher's expectations. If the best student in each Task group scored ten out of ten, which piece of student work would be more valuable?

Then there's the question: How effective is the guidance offered on students' work? It also has to be proposed that fewer really well-marked pieces of work with in-depth guidance for improvement have to be worth more to advance student progress than many more pieces of work scrappily marked with meaningless remarks like 'Well done' or even 'Not your best work'. Ethical marking is about the thoroughness and perceptiveness of the guidance given.

There are also variables which come into play. Knowledge of the student is one such. A teacher may realise that Student A has worked their metaphorical socks off to produce a piece of work; the end-product may only merit a six out of ten grade, but the teacher hopes to encourage the student by giving the piece a seven. Is this then a 'fair' mark? Is it actually 'unfair' to other students who get a seven for work which is worth seven? Is it even 'fair' to Student A, who might believe he/she is better than they really are?

One answer to this is to set marking criteria, and this is arguably an equitable, and therefore ethical, thing to do. Before a task is set, the teacher sets out how marks will be awarded to the completed work. But this approach, while useful, may not be the whole solution. It is quite straight-jacketed: e.g. what reward is there for the student who comes up with a brilliant idea, which is outside the criteria? It could be argued that such an approach might work reasonably well when students are working towards the relatively closed assessments of public examination but are less effective in inculcating the kind of thinking within learning which this text has promoted.

Identifying closely-defined criteria is attractive and looks 'fair' on the face of it. But do criteria work?

To avoid any particular curriculum area or school system, let me give you an example from my time as a university trainer – the level of work really isn't relevant to the argument, what matters are the principles on which criterion-based assessment operated. In this example the students wrote assignments and were awarded marks for each element, e.g. 'Statement of the problem', 'Academic reading and discussion', 'Formulation of a research proposal' and so on. Simple, you might think: just say how many out of ten for Statement, how many for Formulation' and so on – then add them up. But does this work?

In order to standardise marking across tutors we met once a year and all marked the same piece of work against the same pre-determined criteria. I cannot recall a time when the mark range across the tutors was narrower than 45–77 for the same item (that's borderline fail to distinction on the system used). Why? Well, within each element there was plenty of scope for the (carefully and tightly drawn-up) criteria to be differently *interpreted* by different markers; across seven criteria this could produce a massive difference in total marks. To make matters worse there was a catch-all criterion, worth 20 points, which was for the 'Overall performance' in the piece of work – and that really did lead to some confusion. (There really were people who thought that the seven criteria could be fulfilled to a high standard while the work itself should be graded as poor overall; and others who thought that poor grades on the seven criteria could still merit a high score on 'Overall performance'.)

Over time, I would judge that my own marking was consistent – i.e. I applied the same criteria in the same way every time – so the relative scores of my marked pieces of work were consistent and they would have rank-ordered students' work reasonably fairly. But ... it certainly bore little relation to the marking of some other tutors on the same course on Standardisation Day, so marks awarded across the whole student group were inconsistent. Nor was I alone in my reservations. Other research [26] has also concluded that, when looking at university students' marked work:

> Results showed strong agreement among the educators on fewer than half of the scenarios presented in this study. These findings suggest that assessment is currently an educational realm without professional consensus.

So, this is a terrible indictment; herein lies a problem for teachers. If you put together a piece of curriculum which clumps together some 'knowledge', you teach it didactically and tell students this 'lump' of information is what they must be able to reproduce, then you prepare closed exam questions which allow only answers from the 'lump' to be rated as correct – if you do all that, then you can possibly say that you have rated students in a consistent way and given them fair marks for memorisation. Basically, that's what happens in many public examinations (no, not in every instance – but the principle is sound). But the outcomes from this testing are a million miles away from *learning and thinking*; they tell you nothing much about individual students' learning and thinking; they discriminate against students who learn and think but may be bored by memorisation and regurgitation.

A metaphor is in order here to show the significance of this last paragraph. No-one would doubt that a knowledge of the Highway Code is crucial to being a good car driver. But as learner drivers we are required to go, very mechanistically, through the Code, to learn its content and to take very mechanistic tests on it. This knowledge would be valuable provided it were applied when people drove (what I mean by that is, that it may have limited value or less value if you used the knowledge only to answer questions in pub quizzes and not to drive, cycle or walk). But the act of knowing the Code, and passing a test in it, does not *of itself* say anything whatsoever about your practical ability *as a driver*; indeed, you could have passed the Code test and have never stepped into a vehicle. Your car sympathy, your ability to read the road, your understanding of planning ahead for hazards is about the practice of driving not about the Code, however many marks you score in the public test and even though knowing the Code will help with these practical skills when you come to learn them.

In the same way, it is possible for a school to put much effort into attempting to be ethical in its assessment processes and to have highly regarded marking policies which intend to give students the best (i.e. ethical) outcomes for their learning and progress. But if the assessment is mis-directed it may mean very little.

What can we say which is genuinely positive about ethical feedback, marking and assessment; what guidance can middle leaders give to their teaching staff which will help them in their work?

- Feedback to students needs to be continuous and constructive, within lessons whenever it is appropriate, to individuals, groups or the whole class
- Work on written classroom tasks needs to be marked promptly – all good schools endorse this value, and may lay down guidelines (e.g. work is marked within a week, or by next lesson – or the time-scales can be identified for specific pieces of work)
- Marking is about identifying the weaknesses in the work so that students can work on these; it is a critical skill and an important process – marking is best when it is insightful and detailed
- Marking is an opportunity to point out what is right about the student's work, to reinforce good practice, and to give praise for a job well done or for significant effort made
- Marking does not need always to include a numerical grade – effective marking distinguishes between commentary and grades, using the latter only when necessary
- Marking is a private process between student and teacher – no student should be pilloried publicly for errors in their work

- The outcomes of marking may be recorded in order to track students' individual progress, but these data then become subject to appropriate data protection measures
- Middle leaders need to identify a range of marking strategies within their departments: teacher marking, self-marking, peer-marking and so on – as a way to make the process interesting and less burdensome
- Middle leaders should monitor marking efficiency, effectiveness and recording, on a regular basis, to ensure its consistency and value
- It is appropriate for middle leaders to hold review meetings with staff from time to time to monitor the progress of each student and take follow-up action if necessary; this should be seen as part of the caring and pastoral process as well as of being aware of academic progress

You might want to add items to this list to suit your own circumstances or to take into account school marking policies. Ethical feedback, marking and assessment include both an eye to process (how feedback, marking and assessment are carried out) and also content (the quality of any commentary given).

ASSESSING YOUR SCHOOL'S HOMEWORK POLICIES

> **Action**
>
> Before you read the next section, prepare your mind by reviewing the school and department homework policies. Consider: why and how homework is set, how it is marked, how records are kept of the outcomes, and what uses and values it has in the progress of the children's learning and thinking. When you have done that, list any problems which arise from the homework policies in the school. Now read on.

THE ETHICAL CASE FOR HOMEWORK?

The third and final theme of this chapter is the issue of homework, and I am reminded of the Vanessa Williams' (somewhat haunting) lyric about saving the best till last: except that, in this case, it isn't necessarily the *best* – it's the most *contentious*; so be prepared and brace yourself.

There's no other way to say this. One glaring question confronts us and we must face it: Should teachers set homework?

By the way, those strange snarling noises in the background are the grinding of teeth by the proponents of homework – the parents desperate for their children to succeed, the SLTs who have spent forever on a homework policy, the teachers who don't think you can cover a syllabus without it, the examination bodies who feel that confining their subject to school time is an affront to human dignity. The sharp intake of breath was all those students who would have loved to have asked the question but didn't dare, because they are the offspring of the 'band as before', as the drunk curate labelled them.

Seriously: why homework?

These are not my answers, but they are answers:

- I want my child to succeed
- Students need to learn the necessity of discipline in planning their own work
- We can't possibly cover the whole syllabus without it – impossible!
- It is a means of reinforcement for knowledge gained in school
- Everyone agrees it's a good thing for children
- It helps inculcate into students the Protestant work ethic
- Marking it gives me a chance to see what's been learned
- Homework develops the disciplines students need for employment
- Homework develops independent learning skills
- It prepares students for employment where they will work 'after hours'

Some strong arguments there? Well, without comment, let's bring in the really big guns next – researchers! Marzano and Pickering [27] did a meta-analysis of research going back sixty years, which purported to establish that there was a case for the efficacy of homework, but they admitted:

> Although research has established the overall viability of homework ... [it] does not provide recommendations that are specific enough to help busy practitioners. This is the nature of research— it errs on the side of assuming that something does not work until substantial evidence establishes that it does.

This is as near as one can get, in research-speak, to saying this research doesn't prove much. It is reminiscent of those TV adverts which go: '89% of women agreed that they would recommend this product to a friend'; then the small print tells you the sample was only 111 women and doesn't tell you they got free samples. As a researcher myself, I might add more tactfully: the doubt about the viability of homework could be because the case is not actually proven, it consists of hints and possibilities with no actual substance. My own review of homework research suggested that there was little conclusive evidence that homework achieved anything significant or anything which could not be achieved in some other way; and a study by Kazmierzak [28] in America in 1994, though dated, made me smile: In an experimental group of students whose homework was not checked by the teacher during the first quarter of the second semester, quarterly grades were down on those whose homework had been marked – by 1%. One per cent – that was the only difference marked homework made in this study! Research, then, doesn't help the pro lobby very much. The only viable line a researcher might take in favour of homework would be: the more time you spend on something, the better you tend to become at doing it; but even there, it might be necessary to add the *caveat* 'until you get bored with it and go stale'.

There is, of course, an opposite set of views which actively puts the case against homework, so we need to balance the debate. Homework is alleged to fail for these reasons:

- Lack of understanding that children need time to be children
- There are better uses of extra-curricular time (clubs, organisations, sports, etc.)
- Students become exhausted by too much of the same learning activity
- Homework is too often badly (even, not) marked by teachers

- Some students have facilities after-school in school; others don't, so it is not a level playing field
- Homework may be redundant in the new technological age – an old-fashioned concept
- There are too many opportunities to cheat or subvert homework, especially in the technological age
- Students may become bored by academic study – even for subjects in which they have an interest – because of over-exposure to it
- The view that homework inculcates good time-management habits is at best unproven
- Inequality of opportunity – many students come from homes where studying is not possible
- Some families can be stressed by their inability to help with homework
- Homework may get in the way of family time or be resented
- Many students will not have basic facilities to tackle homework effectively
- Homework which is too arduous in content or quantity may add to existing feelings of failure
- Failure to understand that homework is not the only/best way of learning beyond school
- Over-zealous parents may push students too hard to excel at homework tasks
- Homework often lacks clear learning intentions
- Most important of all, homework and homework outcomes may provoke tensions within homes that do not value education.

To me, these arguments are more compelling than those in favour of homework. But, having put them to you, I would like to return to and comment on the case for homework:

- I want my child to succeed (*Most parents do, but is this the best, most equitable, way of doing it within the context of our society?*)
- Students need to learn the necessity of discipline in planning their own work (*In any effective school, students already get plenty of practice of planning and organising work within the school setting; this point is largely spurious*)

- We can't possibly cover the whole syllabus without it – impossible! (*This may be true; but isn't that beginning the problem from the wrong end? Why not devise a syllabus which fits into school time?*)
- It is a means of reinforcement for knowledge gained in school (*There is some truth in this – it can be; but should there be a need for this? If the syllabus is overloaded, see above*)
- Everyone agrees it's a good thing for children (*No, they don't actually; and students don't agree either*)
- It helps inculcate into students the Protestant work ethic (*In so far as this is a virtue, there are better ways to do this – try voluntary service, a cadet force, or part-time employment for older students*)
- Marking it gives me a chance to see what's been learned (*Sorry, but feedback is a continuous process not something separate to be engineered outside the school gates – this is a failure of professionalism*)
- Homework develops the disciplines students need for employment (*See above*)
- Homework develops independent learning skills (*No more than well-planned and executed lessons do – why is more of the same meritorious? Unless the person who says this is implying that all school-based learning is totally teacher dominated?*)
- It prepares students for employment, where they will work 'after hours' (*Some will, most won't; and there is an ethical issue here about compulsion to work more time than one is paid for; and a mental health issue about the detrimental effects this has*).

In a book on the subject, Kralovec and Buell (2000) [29] came to this conclusion:

Homework disrupts families, overburdens children and limits learning.

They could have added:

It is socially divisive.

To be clear, I will say it in plain words – unequivocally; ethically and educationally, there is no compelling justification for homework.

Table 6.1 Planning a lesson with an eye to ethical outcomes

Segment	Lesson plan for (date) (time) (class)	Ethical intentions
TITLE	ROMANS IN BRITAIN: COMPARING ROMAN LIFE WITH OUR OWN	
Intentions	1 To discover aspects of Roman daily life in 1st Century AD: Specifically – town planning, the army & the household 2 To compare/contrast their ways of handling these issues with our own 3 To examine some of the underlying values that emerge	Identification of shared/contrasting values Keeping an eye on the historical evidence to ensure 'truth' (reliability)
Context	Part of the 'Study of Roman Britain' project for Project Week The class has covered some of the invasion history: two invasions; key geographical locations; British tribal boundaries, etc	
Learning and teaching methods Differentiation of methods	Intro/revision – didactic/ lower order questions Class divided into three groups for investigative task: Roman town planning, army and household Students to prepare short expositions to share with the other groups (promotes use of language; technical language and explaining skills) Critical viewing of PowerPoint – teacher higher order questions draw out skills of analysis, application, evaluation and synthesis from the PP	The whole of this task has ethical implications, e.g. town planning matches some modern towns (Milton Keynes) and implies civic duty; army service long and brutal but non-Romans rewarded with citizenship; household chores rely on slaves but again many slaves were freed and gained high ranks in society

(Continued)

Table 6.1 (Continued)

Segment	Lesson plan for (date) (time) (class)	Ethical intentions
	Reinforcement task – making a list of similarities between our life and Roman life with respect to the topic you studied Final thought with which to send class away	
Content and resources	Resources prepared for the three groups: **Town Planning** for competent readers **Army** for able students and faster workers (more ground to cover and more conceptual) **Household** for the slower readers	Resources mirror above intentions
Key questions	If you had been a 1st C Roman in Britain how do you think you would have been regarded by the native population? Why? What would you have most admired about Roman life in 1st C Britain? We sometimes talk about 'life being cheap' in some societies, meaning we don't value individual people all that much; to what extent do you think the Romans thought like this? Why do you think that?	This higher order questioning asks students to explore the Roman values
Task(s); task objectives; Differentiation of tasks	Differentiation carried over from the in-class tasks; but the same basic task for all three groups, which avoids labelling.	Teacher tries to keep students working similarly while taking account of the inevitable differences in ability; the task itself has an ethical element

ETHICAL LESSON PLANNING, ASSESSMENT AND HOMEWORK **97**

Table 6.1 (Continued)

Segment	Lesson plan for (date) (time) (class)	Ethical intentions
	Task objectives for each group: to discover Roman practice/attitudes/achievements; to compare & contrast these with today's; to begin to make an assessment of Roman society in Britain TASK for follow-up lesson: From your study of town planning/the army/ or the household, make as detailed a list as you can of elements of Roman culture which are mirrored in our own. In some ways, we and the Romans seem to have shared similar life-styles and organisation – but do you think we shared the same values? Give some reasons for your answer.	
Assessment	Teacher will comment later on each student's work, trying to ask at least one provocative question about each set of answers	These comments are designed to aid 'values thinking'
Plenary, feedback, and conclusion	At the end of the lesson, the Teacher will prepare the students for a visit next week to the remains of a Roman town where they will see some of the key features on the ground, and be able to trace its layout, how it was guarded by the army, and visualise how people would have lived in it. She tells them there are tourist shops there, so she teaches them a Roman proverb (in Latin)	*Caveat emptor* – Buyer beware

7

ETHICS AND E-LEARNING

A couple of years ago, I had the good fortune to be asked to contribute to a conference for Maltese teachers. This chapter is an updated, but shortened and adapted version of my talk on that occasion, which was a delightful event for me on two counts. In the audience were many former higher degree students whom I had tutored in aspects of education leadership; and the backdrop was the beautiful, tiny, sun-drenched city of Mdina with its quiet streets, honey-coloured city walls, and the migrating warblers picking over the insects in the bushes next to where two farmers were planting potatoes. The theme of the talk was about the ethical challenges which e-learning makes on teachers and on students. The juxta-position of the place and the theme mirrors the old-new worlds in which we all have to live.

LEARNING THROUGH TECHNOLOGY

Effective Information and Communications Technology (ICT) use and e-learning require teachers to harness the potential of the media in ways which enhance pupils' learning and internet usage, and not to use the technology in ways which subvert learning. For example, e-learning has the potential to increase dramatically the evidence to which students have access (compared with old-fashioned textbooks or teachers' notes); but that evidence can come from many sources, and may be accurate, erroneous, or deliberately biased. Furthermore, the ease with which technology is available can create laziness rather than increased investigative diligence. A few minutes before I wrote this paragraph I noticed a query on Twitter, someone asking for information about a particular British bird; the enquirer could just as easily have found out by a few moments' searching on the Web but chose to get someone else to do the work. In the school context, at least, a case can be made that e-learning is not a new model of learning but simply an enhancement to existing models (some of which have been discussed in Chapters 4, 5 and 6).

E-learning media now change almost daily, and the proliferation of updated smart phones and tablets are symptomatic of this. These developments are sufficiently significant that it is clear they are altering our society in a variety of ways. A few examples will suffice. Media outlets/TV companies increasingly rely on opportunistic amateur reporters to provide immediate images for the rolling news; Satnav and Google Earth deliver a whole new perspective on maps, geography and outdoor pursuits; Apps provide information within the palm of the hand on everything from the destination of a plane flying overhead to tomorrow's weather; instant communication via phones and tablets will change our pupils' concepts of work and employment, and in adulthood, their notions of everyday living. We've all been to a bank and not been able to transact business: if a computer goes down, commercial life stops. Even more concerning is the capacity of technology to collect data about us.

The problem for teachers is that, in incorporating technology into lessons, they may operate theoretical models only subconsciously. The problem of e-learning replacing face-to-face lessons was thrown into sharp relief by the Covid-19 lockdown, where students were unable to access schools. Technology was an obvious aid to keeping students learning, but it was used with very mixed success across the involved school populations. These are just some of the questions to be asked:

- E-learning can support a range of learning models but how can we ensure that the choice of e-learning tools reflects rather than determines the pedagogy of a course?
- How do we know that e-learning is an appropriate enhancer of learning in any given situation; or that it is the best way to achieve the educational intention?
- How can e-learning be integrated with other forms of learning, so that it becomes the tool rather than an end in itself?
- What are its pedagogical advantages and (critically) disadvantages?

E-LEARNING AND ITS EFFECTS ON STUDENTS

The point has been made that recent students have made up the first generation of students to be global publishers (because they can share their work online), and that in the process they develop social skills through IT-collaboration – even though they will never meet their collaborators. These students see school as a global communications' centre. We live in an increasingly fact-based society to which technology, arguably, gives pupils a key. Teachers themselves have claimed that blogging, photo-sharing and other IT skills would aid them in understanding how new literacies could be integrated into classroom learning. Research evidence is sometimes produced to say that students prefer learning which is technology based. So it is interesting to note that during the 2020 coronavirus lockdown in the UK, only a small percentage of students accessed the online materials that were provided for them by schools. On the other hand, very many young people and their parents raved about the mathematics learning materials which Carol Vorderman [30] markets online but gave for free during the crisis. What this might be saying is something about the quality of materials: it could be saying something about teachers as celebrities, or celebrities as teachers – but my suspicion is that the major factor is the quality and accessibility of the resources.

But what should we make of the statement that the internet gives everyone – pupils and adults – access to immeasurable quantities of information (data, content)? These data leave open some important ethical debates about e-learning, only some of which can be dealt with here:

- How valuable (authentic, reliable) are these data?
- What are the implications for curriculum of all these data?
- How do these data advantage cross-curricular approaches (see below) to learning?
- What do these quantities of data tell us about the nature of knowledge (epistemology)?
- Are there implications embedded in the data, or in our answers to these questions, about how children should be exposed to all this information?
- What are the resulting ethical dilemmas which emerge from this growing form of learning?

> **Action**
>
> Before reading on, think about your own curriculum and teaching approaches. To what extent have you in your own teaching, and within your department or subject area, taken on learning through e-media? What has been your experience? What have been the advantages? What evidence do you have of improved learning? What about the downsides? What problems have been thrown up?

LEARNING ISSUES

In the light of what has been said so far, and your own experience as a teacher or middle leader, let us review some of the learning issues surrounding technology in the classroom.

Data

We have seen the exponential growth in data (in philosophical terms there may be distinctions between information and data; but in common parlance the words are used interchangeably). Teachers often refer to students accessing these data as being engaged in 'research'. Research is a term best left for finding new things and breaking new ground. What the Web does for most people most of the time is to provide a simple means of access to existing information. The Web can be an excellent means of initial data/information collection.

- Data collection is only a stage – in thinking terms, a fairly low-order thinking operation (see Chapters 4 and 5) – in the process of learning. Students should be encouraged to avoid bad habits. Data which are merely cut-and-pasted have no life in the minds of the students; the information is not theirs, it is someone else's. There are also question-marks about whether this found material is consistently reliable and authentic (see below).
- Data collection gives access to a world of thought which involves: sifting, comparing, contrasting, following new leads, checking contradictions, analysing, synthesising, making judgements, and evaluating. These are higher-order thinking tasks. The Web is best used to feed these higher-order operations, not to replace them.

- All Web searches should be set against the clearly stated objectives for that lesson or learning activity.
- At best, classroom tasks should be so structured that the Web is used as a tool, not as an end-product.

Curriculum

The sheer volume of data available via the internet raises questions about the nature of content, information and data in the curriculum. There are those who believe that 'knowing' or memorising information is an important part of 'education'. A neat definition of memorisation is 'learning an isolated fact through deliberate effort'. Isolated 'facts' may or may not be understood, linked to other knowledge, contextualised – and may not even be accurate. There are immediate *non sequiturs* in this position. What is worth memorising? Who decides what is worth memorising? What is the importance of memorisation and regurgitation when there is instant access to the information anyway? Martinus Hendrikus Benders [31], the contemporary Dutch poet, expresses this educational truth, in somewhat extreme language; but hits the target:

> None of these [higher order learning skills] are taught in our schools, on the contrary the system focuses on memorising. Memorising is a way of overloading the mind with mental baggage it doesn't really need. Besides being horribly dull and stiffening, the effect of 20 years of abundant memorisation training is modern man: an unimaginative creature stuffed with useless knowledge and unable to clean his mind of this information dirt: our school systems are purposely constructed to deliver mental automatons that are unable to think creatively.

But the deeper problem is about epistemology: what is the relationship between 'knowing something' and the kind of knowing which includes understanding, appreciation, context and potential application, in fact a whole range of cerebral activities which have very little do with (but which go far beyond) 'knowing something' in the limited, shorthand sense of memorising de-contextualised 'facts'?

These are not dilemmas with instant and cleanly soluble answers, but they are ethical questions in need of answers.

Cross-curricular approaches

There can be little doubt that the information garnered via the World Wide Web is not, for the most part, filtered through the colander of conventional subject dimensions; and that the quantity of data on any given topic almost ensures that many different approaches will be adopted across the sources, often within an individual source. For the most part, then, web-based data are not predicated on subject boundaries; and they tend to support enquiry-based learning. These are intrinsically positive things; but these characteristics make it imperative that there is an interchange of understanding generated here between the student and the data: first, that the form of the data discovered in response to any individual query is likely to come in formats which support integrated knowledge; and that the student may need to respond (compile, sift, edit, evaluate) those data in a way which takes on board their essential cross-curricular and integrative nature. This is an approach which requires more critical, higher-order thinking; students need to be made ready for this.

Epistemology

The way that pupils receive knowledge in a classroom is dependent, at least in part, on the view which their teachers hold about the nature of knowledge: epistemology. This text has argued throughout that knowledge requires integration to be fully useful (see Chapter 5).

Teaching and Learning

Beyond the use of the Web for access to data or information, it is generally believed that almost all young people respond to ICT in a positive way and are motivated by the inclusion of ICT-related activities during lessons; they are particularly motivated by the whole-class aspect of ICT in learning and teaching, where, for example, a data projector is used, leading to good discussion and high levels of engagement. There is now a multiplicity of means to learn through technology from intra-net access to the school for homework tasks to class blogs and wikis. Many observers note that the commonest uses of ICT are for word processing; and there is nothing wrong with this purpose. But, once more, such a use reduces the computer simply to the status of a tool and underuses its learning potential. To raise its value above this, it is important to have applications which make demands at higher-order levels of thinking: solving design problems, writing stories, producing leaflets and so on.

> **Action**
>
> This might be a good time to review any policies which your school or your department has which deal with technology, especially with technology in learning contexts. Here are some questions to start your thinking:
>
> - What policies are in place?
> - How effective are they in use?
> - Do they deal with learning (thinking and understanding – as opposed to memorisation or fact-collection) not just with process?
> - Is there a coherent view of what learning through technology really means?
> - How might the policies be improved?
> - Do the policies deal with ethical issues?
> - What are the issues, and how do the policies deal with them?

OTHER ISSUES

We have taken a fairly general look at e-learning so far in this chapter, with a few glances towards the ethical issues this throws up. The time has come now to harden up the ethical interrogation of technology and e-learning in schools.

The problem of gaming

A specific subset of ICT activity is gaming. All the same kinds of issues that relate to the use of IT-based learning apply equally to video-games and gaming; but concerns might be deemed to rise in number and severity. Young people and even those up to adulthood are now being exposed to a bewildering variety of games of varying degrees of fantasy from Pokemon, through Football Manager to a plethora of survival games with sci-fi, violent and conflict-driven content. While not all school students will be involved in the undesirable end of this spectrum, commercial pressure and, in unfortunate cases, unsuitable parenting pre-dispose them to potential dangers.

Research has suggested that boys played computer games for more hours than girls but that all those who played tended to become more aggressive, to confront teachers more, and to lower school achievements. However, there may be gains in motor skills and visual attention. On the face of it, a more promising study emanated from Glasgow University [32], involving 11,000 children, but important aspects sometimes ignored in these researches are the psychological dimensions such as whether children confuse fantasy with reality more readily as a result of extensive gaming. At best one can say that the jury is still out on this dilemma, and teachers should approach with caution.

AN ETHICAL APPROACH TO INFORMATION TECHNOLOGY

As hinted at in the ACTION above, there need to be guidelines for the use and application of IT in educational settings. IT has massive potential for expanding informational and social horizons, for accessing second-hand experience, for acquiring and practising specific skills. In itself it is value-neutral. But it has dangers – some obvious, some darker in their implications. What is needed is an informed and ethical approach to its use:

- **Behaviour of individual students** – when using e-mail or other communications media, the rules of truth, manners and personal respect apply just as they do in the classroom, the playground or the dining room
- **Confidentiality** – passwords and other personal information should be safeguarded
- **Plagiarism and the use of sources by students** – merely copying material is stealing or plagiarism, and good habits in this regard are best inculcated from an early age

- **Teacher IT behaviour** – full professional confidentiality and behaviour are appropriate online at all times, just as they are in the face-to-face world of personal relationships.

ETHICAL PROBLEMS FOR E-LEARNING

Relationships and professionalism

A fundamental theme of ethics in e-learning, like ethics in society, is about relationships: teacher-student, student-student, student/outside agencies via the Web. In terms of teacher-student relationships, the teacher is no longer the only source of learning/guidance. Whereas once the teacher either delivered the information or pointed to the (chosen) source (typically a text) which would provide it, now roaming the Web puts the student in touch with other, perhaps contradictory, ideas and information (in spite of technical safeguards operated in schools and by Local Authorities). Unlike the class text, internet data may or may not be shared with other students or the teacher.

This, of itself, raises ethical issues. Whereas, in a conventional lesson, the teacher might be thought to be acting professionally in selecting 'quality' material, vetting its content, checking its relationship to the syllabus/curriculum, guarding the student from erroneous ideas, and acting *in loco parentis* in terms of exposure to desirable/undesirable information, now the role of the teacher in these processes is substantially diminished. So the teacher is left with a series of dilemmas – about his/her professionalism, concerning the extent to which he/she can be a 'gate-keeper' of desirable knowledge (and, thus, attitudes), about his/her subject expertise (once a *sine qua non*), and about the extent to which he/she can guide the understanding of each student in relation to the materials discovered.

Much of the literature refers to this process as if it were a simple case of the teacher slipping out of the preceptor's costume (in which there is implicit a high level of control) and donning the mantle of facilitator. But it goes much deeper than this. The simple act of shifting the student's source from pre-determined text to internet has altered dramatically a whole other range of issues.

SOME IMPLICATIONS OF EDUCATIONAL TECHNOLOGY

> **Action**
>
> As a middle leader, make an opportunity for your team to discuss the following key questions about the implications of the use of technology in teaching. All of these questions include ethical dimensions which are important for all of us as professionals:
>
> - Can the teacher be held responsible, be accountable or given credit in the same way as before for the learning success of the student?
> - Are parents and the public reasonably able to expect to hold the teacher to account for exposing their children to opinions which some individuals might consider inappropriate?
> - Can either head teachers or parents expect to demand specific academic standards from the students as a result of the teacher's work?
> - How might teachers' professional organisations want to re-define professionalism in an era where teachers have lost significant elements of control over knowledge transmission?
> - How might Ofsted and the Government formulate its criteria for judgement of professional performance in these changed circumstances?

Loss of control for teachers/students is also a loss of power. If knowledge is power then the internet rules by virtue of its excess capacity over the human brain. In this context, if the teacher becomes facilitator, then he/she is the servant and the internet becomes the master. Teachers need to develop a far stronger identity as mediators of understanding, interpretation and judgement rather than knowledge-vessels.

Epistemology re-visited

As we have seen, this discussion is both about relationships and communication, but also about the resulting power and the ownership of knowledge. If one accepts its validity, it brings us neatly back to the issue of epistemology. Put simply, it poses the questions:

- Which facts/knowledge/data are reliable?
- Whose facts/knowledge/data are reliable?
- How do we know?

What emerges for the more intelligent e-learner is a healthy scepticism about all the information which is streamed at him/her. The fundamental skill is not to learn it but to interrogate it. Only when its true nature has been explored can it be absorbed into one's *psyche* as being intellectually and ethically sound. However, within the process of finding this discernment, and the knowledge to which it will be applied, lie pitfalls largely unique to e-learning, and these revolve around three concepts: privacy, monitoring and surveillance.

Privacy, monitoring and surveillance

Privacy tends to be delineated by what tutors know/need to know about their students. It has been defined as:

> Freedom from intrusion into the private life or affairs of an individual when that intrusion results from undue or illegal gathering and use of data about that individual. Privacy provision techniques may include controlling the unauthorised copying or gathering of information or controlling transfer of information (Jerman-Blažič and Klobučar, 2005) [33].

Social media sites leave both students and teachers exposed at an extra-curricular, social level (as we saw in a previous Scenario). In school contexts there is a certain amount of data collected by the school which will be available across members of staff in different classes or departments. In ethical terms, staff and students are normally required to follow a confidentiality code which should prevent the trading of personal data. Teachers would do well to familiarise themselves with requirements in this regard.

Nevertheless, it seems the prevalence of cyber-bullying has increased. Since schools have an ethical responsibility for the safety of children, the common response to cyber-bullying often comes in the form of policy, with guidance, sometimes backed by the government about how the issue will be dealt with by the school.

Sound privacy procedures may or may not prevent some monitoring resulting from e-learning, whether this is directly by the school (the collection and collation of performance results for internal use) or through the acquisition of personal data by means of careless practice by the young person when online or as a result of hacking. More important, perhaps, is the increasing (some would say, insidious) collection of data about individuals which happens outside one's control. When I type in my name to book an appointment at the optician, they already have my address on their database; Amazon sends me suggested book titles for purchase based on my previous buying habits; the supermarket loyalty card analyses my shopping; the Government is proud to have notices on the side of vans and elsewhere indicating that illegal immigrants, road tax dodgers or whatever are being monitored and there is 'no escape'. Somewhere, this continuum of privacy – or lack of it – spills over through monitoring into surveillance.

Though surveillance may be IT-based, a common manifestation might be through the use of video cameras to ensure the security of the school site or areas of it.

ETHICAL PROBLEMS IN E-LEARNING MATERIALS' PRODUCTION

There are many potential ethical minefields in the production and use of e-learning materials.

The student problem is that of plagiarism – the ability to download the work not just of academic sources but of other individuals (sometimes for payment) in order simply to cheat in the production of an assignment. Plagiarism occurs when material is used directly and without acknowledgement. It is less of a problem than it might be because technology has kept pace through the use of programmes like *Turnitin*, which monitor students' texts in detail for traces of usage of unacknowledged sources. But there remains a steady stream of cases which slip through the net or are so blatant that they need disciplinary intervention.

In the United Kingdom, research suggested that plagiarism started as early as Year 7, though it is likely that undergraduates are the group most affected. But the statistics raise concerning questions about the ways in which young people construe honesty: whether it is legitimate to cheat in life, whether schools are considered 'fair game' for dishonesty even when honesty might guide other transactions? Or there may be other, different, questions: about whether there is too much homework and students feel under pressure from an early age, or whether society's own norms have slipped in such a way that honesty is no longer seen as a pre-requisite of good citizenship.

A problem for staff – which has emanated from the Higher Education sector, but which will inevitably spread – is that of intellectual commons; or to put it more honestly, perhaps, ownership. The descriptor 'intellectual commons' seems to have been abandoned in recent times for the less insidious Open Educational Resources, defined by the Hewlett Foundation as 'the simple and powerful idea that the world's knowledge is a public good and that technology in general and the World Wide Web in particular provide an extraordinary opportunity for everyone to share, use, and reuse knowledge'. A school might say to a teacher: we pay your wages; therefore, everything you produce (lesson notes, PowerPoint presentations, lesson resources) belongs to us and must be placed in the public domain. But, although these items are produced 'in the firm's time', the fact remains that they are a distinctive part of the individual educator's skills, abilities, techniques and style. To take these over and put them into common and uncontrolled usage is in a very real sense a theft of, and from, the person. The ethical dilemmas presented by this clash of philosophies, by employers wanting to safeguard their 'investment' and individuals wanting to retain their professional integrity, would provide a book-full of debates by themselves.

ETHICS IN THE LIGHT OF CLASSROOM TECHNOLOGY

The purpose of this chapter has been to trace how e-learning challenges the philosophy of education to adapt to a new era. In the process we have uncovered not just new practice but new dilemmas. The solutions are far from simple, but they are in your hands. The absolutely critical questions are about how to make students more critical interpreters of written and visual material, how to encourage them to interrogate data so that they are not duped by it, and how they can retain their own integrity in the face of so much, and such freely available, material which is so open to exploitation, dishonesty and vested interest.

8

ETHICAL CAREER PATTERNS

UNDERSTANDING YOURSELF: THE FIRST STEP TO AN ETHICAL CAREER

This chapter and the next belong together, though they deal with somewhat different topics. This chapter is concerned with establishing an ethical approach to career patterns in teaching, and it adopts two perspectives: the kinds of ethical career path which might be open, and the degree to which achieving them might throw up ethical dilemmas. In the next chapter, Chapter 9, we look at the promoted path of leadership (beginning and middle leadership) in educational settings, and the ethical dilemmas which beset the leader in school situations once he/she has been appointed.

Maybe a good way to begin this chapter is with some self-analysis since, as educationist Margaret (Meg) Wheatley hints, reflection is key to avoiding unintentional outcomes and failure to achieve [34]

Action

Consider each of the following self-assessment questions; answer honestly; hopefully the answers will illuminate what follows in the chapter.

- What motivated you to enter the teaching profession?
- What ambitions do you have for yourself five years, and ten years, down the line?
- Write a pen portrait of yourself in 150 words identifying your ideals in life and in professional life.
- Who, from real life, is your role model character and why?

> - Who, from fiction (TV, literature, the media, the internet), is your role model character and why?
> - If you had to choose one word by which to describe your character, what would it be?
> - What short phrase most accurately sums up for you what you want out of life?
> - What, in your present employment, would you most like to change?

ETHICAL APPROACHES TO JOB SEEKING

The ACTION has given you a systematic chance to begin to 'place yourself' in terms of your values, beliefs and aspirations. This self-knowledge may help in your choice of job applications and in completing application forms. A typical teacher might serve a shortish spell in an initial job, learning the ropes and maybe making a few errors out of inexperience. He/she might then look for a post in a larger or more challenging school where it would be possible to start confidently. This might be followed by a low-level leadership role, maybe second in a department; then by a job as leader of a subject, department, faculty or phase. There are options here to move around and gain experience. You will find yourself, if you are on this career path, filling in application forms, attending interviews, being unsuccessful in your applications, and ultimately being successful and having to face the challenge of an entirely new role (this last is discussed in Chapter 9).

This text does not set out the parameters for ethical procedures for staff appointments: these are controlled by Employment Law. You can Google *Staffing and Recruiting: advice for schools* at Gov.UK for standard procedures. But don't be too surprised, though, if things do not always run according to the strict letter of the law (if they don't, you have rights of appeal but it's not a step to be taken too lightly – usually, you will just chalk any minor malpractice up to experience). A few cautionary tales might indicate that not everything in the appointment business is ethical, let alone straightforward.

To illustrate this last remark, you will discover, for example, that there are still members of interviewing panels who do not appreciate or follow the official guidance. It is not unknown to be asked questions like: 'What do you do with your children when you come to work?' Sometimes an interviewer with political leanings will try to probe yours: one interviewer apologised to me for not wearing a **red** tie. In another example, a colleague was interviewed for a post: the venue, a hotel. Unfortunately, the hotel did not have enough conference rooms so had improvised with bedrooms, pushing the beds up against the walls to make temporary interview spaces. My colleague was successful and later worked with one of the interviewers, who told him that he (the interviewer) had politely apologised to another candidate for interviewing in a bedroom. This other candidate had sought to be humorous and replied: 'It's not the first time for me, but not usually for this kind of job'. He wasn't successful.

At the application stage for any new job – even a first job – part of the task will be to read the job description and person specification, and to construct an application that attempts to persuade others that you are the one best suited for the role. Herein lies your first ethical challenge: to present yourself honestly and with integrity within the constraints of the job description (the ACTION above will have helped you). If you can't do that, don't compromise and don't apply. Remember, that selection for a job ought to be a two-way process: the potential employer will want to vet you; it is equally important that you make a robust decision as to whether this job is the very best for you.

A word of warning, perhaps, to those of you trying to get a first job after training. Almost all training institutions now supply their alumni with model letters of application. Let's imagine a school in location A, somewhere quite close to the training institution. The school advertises and gets ten applications: five from various locations around the country, and five from the local training institution. All of these last five applicants use the same template letter of application, which all end up virtually identical because the writers have simply followed the model without modification. In terms of the appointing panel, this compromises all of the five candidates involved. Personal integrity might suggest that template letters are used only as a guide and perhaps should exist as headings-only documents so that applicants cannot merely reproduce them with minor changes of wording. One could put ethical question marks against the practice of the use of template letters by candidates. The practice is probably ethically questionable from the point of view of the training institution too: it may suggest that their alumni are not capable of producing their own letters, or that they are only peas-in-a-pod with no individuality.

One of the temptations of interviewing panels is to 'adjust' person criteria after they have met the short-listed candidates. So, an applicant turns up for a mathematics' post, let's say; but it only emerges in interview that this person is a genuine expert at amateur dramatics. The head thinks this quality would suit the school well, but it wasn't listed in the person criteria – and the applicant is certainly not the best mathematician. The head might be keen to bend the rules, but technically cannot do so. At best, the post might be re-advertised with changed criteria.

Another issue is properly researching the posts one applies for. Jo went for a job a very long way from home. The closing date for applications was near at hand; pressure of work meant she could not visit the location before she posted the form, and she was unfamiliar with the geographical area. Ethically, maybe she could have done a better internet search, but she didn't. She did, though, travel down the night before to make sure she was at the interview bright and early. Jo was a town girl; the Local Education Authority was called by the name of the nearest city; but when she arrived at her overnight hotel she realised that the school was in a location that was about as out-of-the-way as England gets. She decided to ring at 9 am, to withdraw and present her apologies to the principal, explaining that rural relocation would leave her bereft. Her integrity drove her decision; but the principal was very angry, even threatening. Luckily, she had an understanding head teacher in her present job.

Sometimes you just know that even though all employment law has been ostentatiously complied with, a job has been set up for an in-house candidate. It happened to me once. I went for the interview. There were only two of us; I was told to ring the next day for the outcome. The principal then explained that he had an internal candidate (i.e. the other interviewee) whom he wanted to promote into the advertised post, but he invited me to accept a second-in-command role. I had finished a contract and was not in a permanent post, so needed money to pay the mortgage – I agreed for the sake of my family, though my heart was reluctant – and I really did feel cheated (used, would have been a good word). A letter of appointment was promised but a phone call came instead. The in-house candidate had accepted the post of head of department; but then the second-in-command appointment had been frozen and was no longer available. Frankly I couldn't have been happier. Why? Because I had exposed the lack of integrity at the heart of this institution; I would have been totally out-of-tune with its ethos.

Sometimes a job description and person specification will be so tightly engineered that it allows no freedom to begin to think about how you might mould into the job and personalise it. A friend told me about a school he applied to somewhere out in the West Country. It was a full two days of interviews – four candidates for day one, with two progressed through to day two. My friend didn't make day two; I expressed surprise because he was very able. Apparently, when he arrived in the school, he was taken to meet the other candidates and he discovered they were like peas in a pod. He may have exaggerated a little, but he swore it was true: they were all of an age, all males, all with dark hair, all with virtually identical experience as far as he could see, all married, all five feet ten tall, all wearing the same pattern dark blue suit, and (he says) all in the same M&S tie. He was so spooked he didn't answer the first day's interview questions coherently.

Interviews can be a minefield, as we have seen; but at some point before the final session the panel will ask you whether you still consider yourself to be a candidate. This is the crunch moment. This is when you really do need to know whether your ethical aspirations can be met within this organisation.

ETHICS IN THE JOB MARKET

It is not unknown for the present incumbent for the post for which you are applying to be part of the appointment process – not on the interviewing panel, but maybe around to meet and greet, and to answer questions. Usually, incumbents (however glad they may secretly be to go elsewhere) are there to praise the post, tell you how wonderful the job will be when you accept it, and generally further the institution's cause of appointment. On one occasion, though, a work colleague of mine was interviewed with three others for a quite prestigious job. On day two, the first scheduled session was a talk from the incumbent about his job and the institution. Candidates gathered in his office. He began the session by saying (I have modified the reported language): 'You will all think this place is the bees' knees and you'll be desperate to take the post. Don't. This is a lousy institution; the management is untrustworthy; the job is rubbish. Prepare now your excuses, so that when they offer it to you, you can withdraw with dignity'. There were a lot of ethical questions here, pretty much unanswerable, because my friend and her fellow candidates had no idea whether the incumbent's motives were courageous and honest, or represented a vicious payback for a personal vendetta. She got through to the last two, and at the crunch question was lucky enough to hit on a reason why she could not take the post which was at least plausible. She still cannot fathom the incumbent's motives.

ETHICAL CAREER PATHWAYS

We have looked now at the processes surrounding ethical employment: at your own assessment of yourself to be conveyed to a potential employer, and at the ethical nature of the employer's procedures for appointing potential employees. It is time to turn our attention to the career path itself: are there ethical paths through a lifetime's career?

Employers who care about their own ethical standards care also about how ethically applicants behave; they may even test them out during the interview process through the use of exercises like the ACTIONS used in this text. They will build up intelligence on institutions from which new employees are drawn. This is harder when the job is a second or third-rung job. An employee who accepts a post and then withdraws in the face of a better offer soon learns that this is a poor career move; it is important to apply only for those roles for which one is suited and keen.

Teachers who seek an ethical career path might do well to take into consideration a number of issues as outlined below:

Ethical ideals: Given that teaching is an ethical profession aimed at the greater good of students, does that mean that the ethical teacher should seek jobs where he/she can do most good? The answer is 'probably' – but the definition of 'most good' is fluid. For example, Miss B is a talented drama teacher but not the most able at class management and finds mixed gender classes a trial. To maximise her abilities, she is probably most suited to an all-girls' school, where behavioural issues are limited, and where she can use her talents mainly on school productions. Mrs H on the other hand, does not have many class management issues, and prefers teaching in a mixed gender situation; she finds both boys and girls respond to her technology lessons. She is not strong in the questioning and investigational elements of lessons, but she is hands-on practical, finds that students like her, and she has a strong caring instinct. She is at home in an average comprehensive, where she does sterling work with some of the less well-motivated. Miss B and Mrs H would each feel like fish out of water if they swapped schools: so, in terms of doing the best for students, they have found their respective niches and their chosen roles are ethical in their individual contexts.

Lifelong adherence to a single job role suits some teachers and not others: Mr P has a very high boredom threshold. He is happy to get a job at St Saviour's village school – after all, he attended there, was a trainee there, got his first job there, and doesn't see any good reason to move as his family are all in the village. For some, this would be a stultifying existence; as someone once said 'not thirty years' experience but one year's experience repeated thirty times'. But the context in which Mr P works likes continuity, and he is happy; he's a competent teacher and does not have much ambition. Ethically, there is no reason, while ever students thrive under his tutelage, he should change his ways. By contrast, Mrs V is a live-wire; she finds it hard to do one thing very long and is bored by repetition. Mrs V knows that the secret of her considerable success as a teacher is her freshness; she re-trains in different skills regularly, is keen to teach new subjects, volunteers as special needs co-ordinator, and wants to use her talents in leadership roles. Ethically, Mrs V's dynamism is what makes her effective, and she recognises her own potential when she exercises this.

Using your skills at different levels in the education profession: Miss L enters the profession as secondary teacher, and enjoys the comprehensive school well enough; but her temperament is to look at the greener grass over the fence – she thinks she might be suited to upper juniors, and trades her post, even taking a bit of a drop in salary. She finds she likes this even more; but after a few years she feels that the breadth of her pedagogical knowledge needs to be matched by an academic qualification, and she completes an MA. With this under her belt, she feels impelled to move into a training role; working in a Higher Education department gives her the chance to research for a PhD and publish her results. After a while she decides that she will join a consultancy that trains the trainers; but the politics of this last appointment are not to her taste. After a couple of years, she decides to return to the classroom and secures a management post in a school. Her career is very varied; has affected a lot of students for the better; has had a wider influence through training trainers who will themselves adopt her ideals and teach them to others; and she can still do a job she loves without losing touch with the grass roots of teaching students. An interesting career, varied, and with plenty of ethical intent.

A career path like that of Miss L is harder to pursue than it once was; that is a tragedy. We all know that the grind of classroom work does wear people down – the profession would be more vibrant if teachers had expanded career choices. Ethically, teachers should probably be able to expect a more varied diet over their thirty-plus years in the job. But governments prefer things like salaries and pensions in neat boxes; it could be argued that teacher unions are more concerned with guarding what they have than expanding individuals. It doesn't do any harm, though, to dream – within the boundaries of realism.

> **Action**
>
> In the best of all worlds, and given your own analysis of your skills and temperament, what kind of a career would you, ideally, map out for yourself? What choices would you make, for what reasons, and to fulfil what ethical principles in your own career planning?

MAKING TEACHING A MORE ATTRACTIVE CAREER OPTION

In reality, we are back to that matter of reflection with which this chapter began. Career exploration focuses on skills; in particular, the importance of identifying your own skills. Combined with this is identifying the central core of your preferred intentions for your career: being able to articulate what motivates you at a deeper level, i.e. your ethical intentions or values. These two processes are transformative: they help to prioritise your work and to make decisions about professional opportunities you want to pursue. But there need to be opportunities available once this process has been completed. UNESCO [35] is currently investigating ways of improving career enhancement for teachers. Their Report, still in its infancy, makes some key points. (I have included a selected few only):

- *A major question for governments is how to transform teaching into an attractive career choice for today's youth.*
- *Many governments are looking for ways to diversify teacher career structures and to widen career advancement opportunities in order to attract and retain high-performing teachers.*
- *A close examination of the organisation and management of teacher careers can provide useful insights into making a teaching career more appealing.* (Interestingly, Scotland is involved but England is not.)
- *A (potential) second-generation structure is the career ladder, in which teachers take on a new status or role after meeting the required standards to do so, with their pay reflecting the new position; the reformed career structure had to include a career ladder which sought to diversify the professional course of teachers and to widen advancement opportunities.*
- *Promising career schemes are expected to motivate teachers 'from the inside'.*
- *Looking at proxy indicators of teacher autonomous motivation, this research finds that, overall, teachers very positively welcome having more opportunities for career progression while still being able to stay in the classroom.*
- *It is all the more important to encourage teacher collaboration, because it is a powerful means for professional development and knowledge sharing within schools.*
- *Well-designed reforms can also have a positive impact on regulating entry into the teaching profession, as well as providing essential support to new educators.*
- *Thanks to the greater selectivity of candidates for the profession, these new requirements helped improve the calibre of the professionals recruited.*

I will end with a quotation from Henry Adams [36], historian and intellectual. He propounded a curiously modern theory of physics as he saw it applying to history – in effect, he said that all energy dissipates, order becomes disorder, and the earth will eventually become uninhabitable. There are many who now agree with him. But his comment on teachers (both male and female) captures the mood of this chapter:

A teacher affects all eternity; you never know where his influence stops.

9

ETHICAL MIDDLE LEADERSHIP

THE IMPORTANCE OF ETHICS IN LEADERSHIP DECISIONS

If you are reading this book, the chances are that you are one of these people: a middle leader in schools, a teacher, or someone who is training to be a teacher. The latter two categories will be, albeit on different timescales, aspiring to be leaders. So this chapter is for all of you at some point in your careers.

So far this text has looked, at times in some detail, at ethical decisions as they affect teachers as professionals, and teachers in the classroom deciding about curriculum content, working out learning and teaching strategies, preparing lessons, assessing students' work and using technology as an aid to learning. Those who are already middle leaders in schools will have been challenged to examine their practice *vis-à-vis* their teams. And everyone will have noted the centrality, in ethical terms, of the student to the thinking of professional educators.

In this chapter, I am going to turn the spotlight of ethical behaviour onto the activities of the middle leaders specifically. It won't be an easy ride in terms of its challenges; but then neither is the role of leader. But first, a couple of quotes to set the scene. The other day, I was in a Regimental Museum, standing in front of a huge case full of gallantry medals won by brave individuals in times past; and it reminded me of a quotation from Mark Twain to the effect that moral courage was much rarer in the world than physical courage [37].

Mark Twain so often touches that depth of perception which takes one's breath away, and he has scored a bull's eye here; Mayur Ramgir [38], author and IT expert, is less pithy, but is right to make, very economically, the point that ethical leadership and an ethical leader belong inseparably together in the humanity of the person who leads:

> Your actions define your character, your words define your wisdom, but your treatment of others defines the REAL you.

ETHICS, YOU AND LEADERSHIP

That insight gives us a neat entrance into the question: What kind of person makes an effective leader?

To be a leader you need to be a person of substance. It reminds me of that biblical passage when Jesus challenges the crowd with an ironical question concerning John the Baptist, and asks them: 'What did you go into the wilderness to see – a reed blown in the wind?' Of course not, they went to see someone who was the top charismatic of their age (though, just maybe, we should remember he came to a sticky end!).

So begin at the beginning: know yourself, and above all your weaknesses. Be comforted that everyone has weaknesses: look for your strengths, too. Work on your weaknesses, but above all, work always towards continuous improvement in your approach and in your skills – there's no room in ethical leadership for the brittleness of complacency. Do everything you do to the best of your ability; but hold the line at becoming neurotic or obsessive. If you can't do something, don't fail – learn. Be a role model to students and colleagues – a role model of learning; learn alongside them too.

You need courage, of course; that moral courage Mark Twain spoke about. Consider this account of needing courage which was unpredictable:

> 'I was asked to give a talk to all the County's primary headteachers, hosted at a school and by a headteacher, Mrs Zee, who were notoriously hostile to my organisation. I had been forewarned by one of the course leaders that Mrs Zee was likely to engineer those present into a very hostile reception. I decided the best adverts for my course were the students themselves; I took along the two course leaders and several students – the latter with their course files so they could show people what they did. We arrived

at the school and were met by Mrs Zee: we had arrived nearer to start-time than I had wished because of traffic, but that played unexpectedly into my hands: the hall was already packed with headteachers. When we entered, Mrs Zee became very challenging. 'Who are all these people?' she asked; and I explained. 'They are not coming in', she raged; 'I asked for a talk from you not your fan-club!' 'Fine', I said, 'but if they go, I go. Before I do, I'll just go and explain to the audience your prohibition; but I won't do the talk without them'. She capitulated in what is known in literary circles as high dudgeon. As I expected, the students were brilliant, and the talk was a great success. At the bun-fight after the meeting, the students were inundated by crowds of admiring headteachers. There are times when you don't have to do the talking yourself.'

> ### Action
> No-one is immune from ethically dubious situations. So this little story is redolent with them. What would you have done? Assess the value of hindsight. Before you read on in the text below, just try to de-construct this event; discover what else you might like to know, probe the motives and events, and make an ethical judgement about it and all the actors in it.

Now, back to you, and to the qualities needed in a leader. It helps to be competent, professional and confident in the role – again, constant training and up-dating will help here. Enjoy responsibility and seek it; things **will** go wrong, but when they do, don't blame others to cover your own misjudgements. Use every incident as a learning process, whether things go well or badly. Over time, develop the skill of making well-judged decisions, but also of making well-timed decisions.

A good leader, like a good teacher, is a role model for others. You don't have to be popular (it may be better if you are not – too many leaders seek social friendship, even acclaim, rather than professional respect). Care about your team – all of them – even the ones you don't much like. A major error in the mind of many leaders is that you have to like someone to work with them. That is not true if you both bring the right approach to the relationship. Good leaders tend to feel loyalty and a sense of responsibility towards their team members; loyalty may, if you are fortunate, be catching but it begins with you. In professional relations there is no room for pettiness. It helps to train and learn with the team, that way goals are shared.

Be aware that leadership brings both money and (more importantly) status. But middle leaders (in fact, everyone in the universe this side of the deity) report to someone else. So understand the conventions of communication, both up and down your particular hierarchy. Professionalism and respect should always guide these interpersonal transactions. But that does not mean you should always agree with those above you; and it certainly doesn't mean that you should act in a superior manner to those below. Know when to give a subordinate their head and to take a risk; know when to pull rank.

But the most important characteristic of the leader in educational organisations is to know where priorities lie. For my mind, in the day-to-day running of a school, they lie with the students. Older notions of leadership were often pictured as a triangle, with the principal at the top and the newest teachers and the students on the bottom rungs. No more. The image is a wheel, and the centre is the student body: after all, that's why we're there! That image will be a first step, every time there is a decision to be made. In this way we are drawn back to the first two chapters of this book: teachers and teacher leaders are there to bring about the greatest good (however, that is defined) for the people who form their clientèle – and they are the students.

At the heart of ethical leadership is not 'Team department', not 'Team staff', not even 'Team school' – it is 'Team student'.

Action

At the heart of ethical leadership is not 'Team department', not 'Team staff', not even 'Team school' – it is 'Team student'.

Examine this statement against what happens in your school context.

At a suitable time, find an opportunity to discuss this statement with fellow middle leaders both inside and outside your institution.

ETHICS AS A FACTOR IN DEFINING LEADERSHIP QUALITIES

So let's now shift the focus of our discussion from what kind of person a leader is, to what qualities they need, and need to display.

Above everything else stand two qualities without which leadership has no validity: integrity and honesty. These are related but different. Integrity implies that a person's life is guided by an underlying philosophy of straight dealing, respect for the rights and dignities of others, and determination to behave in ways that are best for others; honesty is about the more immediate quality of telling the truth. Or, as Heather R. Younger, founder of Customer Fanatix, explained: ethical leaders exist for integrity – they live by the code of doing the right things whatever the cost.

How can anyone aim for this ideal in the context of educational leadership? Perhaps by adopting these qualities as their habitual *modus operandi*:

Honesty: because honesty and integrity go hand in hand. This may lead to some difficult decisions; there are times when telling the whole truth may be painful to the hearers. Imagine the problem of informing a group of staff about the decision to lower the profile of their subject area by cutting back its timetable slots or confining it to the sixth form only; or breaking the news to a part time colleague that their work will cease in the new academic year. The same honesty must extend to students, to ensure they have realistic hopes and aspirations.

Respect: A multifaceted quality which ranges from accepting that others may legitimately hold different opinions from one's self, through acceptance of different cultural norms, to understanding deep professional divisions about how best to teach a topic. The skill of listening is important in the leader, even if the team member's views cannot be accommodated. Students, above all, should always be respected as individuals, their strengths recognised.

Humanity: Personal relations with the team and with the leader might be characterised by personal concern for all team members and an understanding of individual frailties. In a team situation, some of these issues may be compensated for by colleagues on a reciprocal basis. This humanity should spill out from the team into their dealings with students, so that students know that staff 'are on our side'.

Just dealings: Students should know that their teachers will be fair in their decisions, and consistent, acting without favouritism or discrimination.

Team skills: Ethical leaders lead from the front when necessary, giving opportunities to others when they can. Initiative is encouraged while support is available. Team members adopt the same approach to students. Ethical middle leaders are role models for team members and students.

Decision-making: Decisions are always made against a background of honesty and integrity. Violations of this code by team members or students are not tolerated.

This paragon of virtue we call the middle leader, then, certainly has something to live up to! Let's try to sum up what that is likely to be in practice from our deliberations about the kind of person who is likely to make an effective and ethical leader, and the qualities which one might expect from them.

This is a person who is not arrogant or status conscious but offers a degree of humility. He/she will respect the fellow team members and try, where reasonable, to balance their views when forming decisions and courses of action. These decisions will take into account the declared values of the school and the team, as well as the leader's own integrity and consistent values. Among these values is honesty, which means that information will be shared and there will be as much open-ness as possible. At all stages, from idea to retrospective view, critical evaluation of situations will be encouraged; that process will be objective, blame-free and in the spirit of academic debate. It must remain clear, though, where ultimate responsibility and decision-making lie: leadership is not about abdication. The leader will encourage the team members themselves by coaching, mentoring and training them with a view to improving the team and its performance – remembering always that the team's focus is their clients, the students.

Action

Given this summary of the nature of the ethical middle leader, imagine you have to write a job advertisement for a middle leader in your school for approval by the headteacher (you can choose a subject area or other area of responsibility). How would the advert look? How might you ensure you got the right kind of applicants given what you know about ethical leadership?

ETHICS AND THE UNCERTAINTY OF LEADERSHIP

The role of the middle leader is ambiguous at times; and it is demanding. Here we consider one of the reasons: the middle leader is answerable to so many people, and all of them have a legitimate claim, yet may have conflicting expectations. Ultimately, the middle leader is answerable to the principal or the head of the school; in the process he/she has a loyalty to colleagues to work in the way which the school designates as the one embraced by the school's vision and mission. These last may well lay down principles for how the job role is to be carried out. But these immediate concerns are augmented by a range of more amorphous controls: most immediately those of parents (operating either face-to-face or through parent governors), those of the employing authority, of government aspirations for education (most obvious during inspections or in league tables of school achievement), and Society – which has its own notions of schools and schooling.

It may be worth remarking at this point that the symbiosis between school and Society is largely sub-conscious but more powerful than may sometimes be credited. It is true that Society gets the schools it deserves, but conversely schools get the Society they deserve too. What does that mean exactly? If Society (usually in the form of another control, e.g. the government or parents) demands too much of schools, or does not support teacher sanctions to control poor behaviour, or puts its educational aspirations in the wrong places, then its schools will reflect those poor judgements. However, when schools fail to deliver (e.g. do not prepare students appropriately for the world of work, or do not convey to students ethical standards by which they might live their lives in Society), then – in the fullness of time – Society itself fails economically or socially.

So middle leaders spin plates: They have to satisfy a range of audiences. First and foremost, they have a duty towards their core clients – the students. But, in the process, they have to lead junior colleagues, answer to senior colleagues, and be aware of the bigger picture as described above. All of these factors require ethical decisions, and ethical behaviour, of the kinds previously outlined in the chapter. But, inevitably, there are times when the conflicts inherent in these ethically-based activities produce tension – more commonly known as stress. The public has become increasingly aware of mental health issues and stress factors in employment, and as individuals we need to safeguard ourselves. Hence middle leaders (like all employees) need a sound approach to work-life balance.

I don't believe that a lay person can give effective advice about work-life balance and elimination of stress, so I am not going to try except in the most general of terms. Experience suggests these might be sound principles on which to operate:

- You know yourself better than anyone knows you and how you feel; if you are constantly weighed down by your role as a middle leader (in other words, the concerns far outweigh the joy of it on a daily basis), you might seriously consider whether you are in the right job: the heat and kitchen syndrome
- If you enjoy your role and love the challenge, you may be in the right role but may still have occasional incidents to deal with which cause you stress; this is normal – be aware of the cause of this specific stress, and deal with it even if it takes a little time
- Have an intelligent approach to working practice: monitor how many hours you work; don't be constantly at everyone's beck and call; learn to say 'No!'
- When it's time to stop, stop. Don't be an over-willing horse or you will become a beast of burden. Take short breaks, and longer vacations: use these to turn off completely
- Above all, learn short-term detachment. Have something you can retreat to for an hour or two when the going gets tough – embroider, learn to play the trumpet, do granny's shopping, run up a fell, photograph lichen, ride a heritage railway, sit in the sunshine with a mug of cocoa, listen to the birds, meditate: whatever turns you on.

ETHICAL CONSCIOUSNESS IN LEADERSHIP BEHAVIOUR

We have to be realistic: Even the most ethically-conscious leaders make occasional bad decisions. They may be relatively trivial and reparable, like snapping at a colleague when we are weighed down with a quite different, confidential matter. That can be repaired with an apology and an explanation, hopefully. Sometimes, we make a big error: the best course is to own up – voluntarily, immediately and without reservation. Your team members will make similar errors: they need your understanding, support and protection too. A habit of mind which stands back and considers a decision, in ethical terms, before rushing into action is to be applauded. Anticipating issues is even better, when possible – it doesn't leave the leader wrong-footed.

An initiative by the Chartered College of Teaching, known as FELE (Framework for Ethical Learning in Education) has made early progress in examining some of the ethical issues affecting school leaders (both FELE and the Chartered College can be Googled, but the information is relatively sparse as yet). It came up with a set of key words which ought to define the leader's behaviour:

- Selflessness
- Integrity
- Objectivity
- Accountability
- Openness
- Honesty
- Leadership.

The chapter, and this text, have clothed these concepts with some detail without always using the identical descriptors, putting a slightly different emphasis on their relative importance, perhaps, and adding some others of equal significance.

But you have chosen your path. You are, or will be, a middle leader. Let's imagine you have moved your leadership role to a new school or have recently obtained your first promoted post; the realities of leadership, or leadership in a new culture, are about to kick in, in practical terms. Read the ACTION below, and then carry it out.

Action

Below is a more detailed scenario than most of the previous ones in this text. Read the scenario carefully in the light of what this chapter has said about ethical leadership, and what previous chapters have outlined as ethical teaching behaviours. With those things in mind, work out a series of strategies to solve the problems you now face as a middle leader. As the task is complicated, record your response on paper; try to find alternative options as problem-breakers wherever possible; identify your priorities, preferred strategies and desired outcomes – and the routes you would take to get there. Match your actions to the ethical principles we have talked about in this text.

Scenario: Taking over a new area of work

You have recently taken over a new department: for the purposes of this exercise you are a linguist (the subject area doesn't matter here but to avoid debates about the merits of which languages should be taught in schools, we will call it the Albanian department). What is more important are your departmental colleagues. You have been in the school a couple of weeks, watched them all at work, been a bit disappointed by the physical area of the languages department, and have seen that the students' grades are disappointing overall and variable across year-groups. You have made a tentative assessment of the three staff:

Tracey is the next most senior member, aged 40+, a disappointed candidate for your job, who has been in the school sixteen years. Her class control is casual; she can be over-familiar with some students. Results are satisfactory at GCSE level but poor beyond that. Her general demeanour is scruffy, her classroom disorganised, and her paperwork only adequate. She has two children of her own (one in the school, and studying Albanian); she is a live-wire in the local amateur dramatic society and has a wide circle of influential friends outside school, including several of the school governors.

Will has had two years' experience. His teaching skills are pedestrian, but he keeps the students on-side because he is very much into sport outside the school day; he meets many of the students socially through his gym. His GCSE results are just about satisfactory, but he gives the impression of being slightly lazy and does not push himself or the students very hard. He is, though, very affable; and his e-learning skills are very good on the occasions when he can be bothered to produce resources.

Jane is the youngest and newest teacher. She has a very good degree, is very crisp and professional in manner, is well-versed in class management, and pushes the students hard. Her aspirations are high, and she can teach at all levels within the syllabus. A live-wire, she is keen to get school trips organised to augment the classroom learning; some of these would be to an Albanian society to which she belongs and which meets at weekends. Her main down-side would appear to be that she has put up the backs of a number of non-languages staff by being very opinionated in the staffroom, and sometimes being a bit too informal with students.

It is Christmas, and you have only months to raise the student grades at both GCSE and GCE levels.

ETHICS AND THE COURAGE TO LEAD

In this ACTION maybe you have been faced with your first real leadership problem to solve. Maybe you have faced other problems but not been faced with a problem of such a demanding nature before. Maybe you have indeed faced similar issues. Perhaps you remember the catch in the throat and butterflies celebrating golden summers in your intestines when you realised the enormity of what you had taken on. Leadership is a complicated issue, full of ethical dilemmas; but if you enjoy living a bit 'on the edge' it is a satisfying career move. If you want to find out more, you could always read my other Routledge volume: *Stand Up and Be Counted: Middle Leadership in Education Contexts* (2021). But let's summarise the chapter with three important thoughts.

John C. Maxwell, the American leadership guru and pastor [39], recognised this butterfly syndrome; he emphasised that the wisest move is to anticipate it, to be prepared: he thought positive fear provoked preparedness, negative fear induced avoidance.

My experience is that leaders who avoid, always avoid: they become bad leaders and usually damaged ones. In many ways, if you enjoy leadership, once you've been a leader, you never quite shake off that lust to explore the new situation, the challenging event, the incident that is handled ineffectually by someone else. You tend to spend your time reflecting on how you might have gone about solving these problems, even though they are not your problems. I bought a leisure shirt which was a bit unusual – and I thought it needed a logo of some kind on it. Then I came across an iron-on patch with one which caught my eye. It was an allusion to J.R.R.

Tolkien [40] and it sums up that leadership wanderlust: *Not all who wander are lost.*

Reflecting on leadership problems, strategies and behaviours is a positive thing. But complicated issues need people who can act incisively. No-one knew that better than Colin Powell [41], the American former four-star general, whose humility and quiet confidence were cut short by ill-health in his subsequent political career. He knew that often leadership was about keeping things simple, that effective leaders were simplifiers who offered followers accessible solutions.

> How is your solution to the Albanian department problem working, by the way?

10

ETHICAL GOVERNANCE

ETHICAL SCHOOL GOVERNANCE: SOME PARAMETERS

This chapter will be quite short but, for the sake of completeness, will deal with another crucial partnership in delivering the ethical school: the school's governing body. Governing bodies work under their own Codes of Practice, different in detail for academies and maintained schools. You can look up this guidance electronically or in hard copy and check for latest amendments:

- From the Department for Education (2017) The Constitution of governing bodies of maintained schools: statutory guidance London: DfS
- From the Department for Education (2019) Governance Handbook London: DfS
- Academy trusts: governance via assets.publishing.service,gov. uk/uploads/system/uploads/attachment_data/file/788234/governance_handbook_2019.pdf

This chapter has three main aims: to locate the governors in the whole ethical framework of the school; to identify how governors can operate ethically; to glance at the role of staff-governors (formerly teacher governors) in this ethical context.

The role of the governing body of a school is best summed up in the role of the Chair of Governors, who will:

- Work with the Head to promote and maintain high standards of educational achievement
- Ensure that the governing body sets a clear vision, ethos and strategic direction for the school
- Ensure that the governing body holds the Head to account for the educational performance of the school and its pupils, and for the performance management of staff
- Ensure oversight of the financial performance of the school, and the effective use of the school's resources.

Item one here recalls our ethical concern to provide the greatest good for all students. In Item two, vision and ethos mirror what has been said earlier about creating a values' culture within the school. Item three shifts the focus to the fundamental role of governors as the quality controllers of the school – asking the head hard questions and focusing attention on any weaknesses, part of the self-examination and reflection required of an ethical school. The fourth item identifies the role of governors in making sure that the school itself operates in a practical way within ethical guidelines: mainly here in relation to financial matters, but implicitly in more general ways too. These few clauses encapsulate the locus of governance in the ethical and values arena.

ETHICAL SCHOOL GOVERNANCE IN ACTION

Ethical governance of schools is controlled by law. However, the National Governance Association (NGA) issues guidance [42], which is detailed and careful, about the practice of school governance. The strategic roles of the governing bodies of schools resonate with all that has been said in this volume about ethical procedures in schools. The Association confirms that the governors have three strategic functions:

- Setting and ensuring clarity of vision, values, and objectives for the school
- Agreeing the school improvement strategy with priorities and targets
- Meeting statutory duties

And it recommends a fourth:

- Ensuring that other key players with a stake in the organisation get their voices heard by gathering and using the views of pupils, parents and staff; reaching out to the school's wider community and inviting them to get involved; using stakeholders' views to shape the school's culture and the underpinning strategy, policies and procedures.

Governance is an important and skilled role; it does not always get a good Press. Several years ago, Michael Wilshaw, the then Chief Inspector of Schools, went on the record to say that governing bodies should not be made up of people who were untrained and did not understand the ramifications of their role. There was, he said, no room for amateurism.

Wilshaw believed that, often, governors devoted too much time to marginal issues such as school uniform, the dinner menu and peeling paintwork, rather than more important matters such as the quality of teaching, pupils' progress and the culture of the school. Add to this that, in some quarters, governors seem to be resented by teaching professionals, who find them either intrusive or irrelevant, and one has to conclude that this is an area fraught with problems.

I have been a member, a Chair, and had consistent dealings with, many governing bodies in schools of different kinds in different phases. My own experience has been that most governors are conscientious, well-intentioned, and very often well-informed and diligent. They bring many skills from the world beyond schools. That doesn't mean that things never go wrong. The most critical moments for governing bodies are probably the appointment of a new headteacher, or the times when the head and governors disagree on a matter of substance. This is not the place to deal with either of these concerns; but it is fair to say that governors can get advice should they need it, and there is no excuse for poor performance in these circumstances.

In day-to-day running, the role of the governors, in a nutshell, is to check on the quality of the school by asking perceptive questions: they hold the head to account. What they do not do, is to run the school. Questions of quality deal with academic and financial issues.

One of the most contentious areas of school life is the school budget. In a large school – maybe a secondary academy – this runs into many millions. There will be someone in the administrative system who looks after the books, and engineers value for money – a bursar or finance manager. But the strategic direction of the spending will be the domain of the principal supported, usually, by a small finance committee involving teaching staff as well as administrators. But one area of ethical failure in schools is, far too frequently, in the handling of public money. There are multiple cases every year of this kind of abuse. Sometimes, an academy head, who has a lot of financial freedom, will spend money without authorisation, maybe on personal rather than school-related costs. It is far too common to read about school finance officers milking money out of the school system for personal use – even, in the process, sometimes committing elaborate fraud to achieve this end.

But financial failings may not be matters of dishonesty but of incompetence: a school may, for example, wish to make better use of part of its grounds. It decides to build some state-of-the-art all-weather pitches, and to re-coup part of the cost by hiring these to the public outside school hours. The Bursar is tasked with contracting the work and, in due course, establishing a lettings' system. After the pitches are installed it is discovered that a spring runs out under them and in inclement weather the ground is unusable. The investment and potential income are both compromised. Inevitably, blame is legally contested between the Bursar, the site surveyor, the civil engineering contractor. The school remains the loser.

STAFF GOVERNANCE: ITS ROLE AND CAREER VALUE

Teachers may be eligible to become governors – formerly teacher-governors, now staff-governors, as non-teachers are also eligible – in their own schools; this is an opportunity which is insufficiently accessed. At the time of writing, the National Association of Schoolmasters/Union of Women Teachers is offering a course for staff-governors; the advertising blurb [43] is splendidly confrontational:

The course tackles some common misconceptions about staff governors and will enable participants to resist attempts to prevent their full participation in the deliberations and decisions of the governing body.

In a similar vein, the *Schools Improvement* [44] web page posts the information that: staff-governors are generally nominated/endorsed by the headteacher – who won't want any dissenters. It advises: always agree with the headteacher – not many individuals would want to disagree with their boss in open forum. It claims (probably quite accurately) that staff-governors have often had little or no governor training, and therefore have limited understanding of the role of the governing body.

Phil Revell, in a Times Educational Supplement rant [45], warns:

> Expect a lot of ... meetings. Not just the governors' meetings, but also the uncomfortable tête-a-têtes with the head that follow those occasions when you were rash enough to wander off message ... A stray comment by a member of staff can trigger all kinds of unintended consequences, from the formation of yet another governors' working party, to the abandonment or delay of one of the head's cherished projects.

Not much to encourage participation in any of that, then. But how valid is it? How accurately does it represent teachers as governors?

In my personal experience, I do recognise the issues set out here relating to teachers' reluctance to become governors. Teachers will do almost anything, even beyond the call of duty, that relates to students and the classroom. But they do not like putting in 'unpaid overtime' on other activities, especially meetings. Governing Body meetings are often overly long; and they do have some potential to compromise individual teacher members if they disagree with school policy. But the NGA comes up with a potential solution, a very good one, and it is this:

Teachers and leaders should become governors of other schools to enrich their professional development; NGA seeks to encourage education professionals to join the governing boards of **other schools or of other academy trusts than their own**. It claims (rightly) that there are enormous professional development benefits to doing so, and teachers and leaders stand to benefit from valuable experience of strategic leadership, including finance and human resources for aspiring leaders.

These claims are absolutely accurate; they should certainly be considered by anyone who is an aspiring leader in education. They provide opportunities to learn about strategic planning, and areas like finance; opportunities which may simply not exist in the teacher's own employment context. As an addendum to the CV, they are potentially very significant. They also provide that important insight into how strategic planning can be used to promote the ethical purposes of the school, and how management of a school can be employed to the greater good of all students.

Becoming a governor in a school other than one's own removes the pressure of being a staff-governor; but let's not wholly rule out teachers as governors. Huntington School in York [46] makes some good points on its web page, and especially that staff-governors are representative members of staff rather than representatives of *the* staff; they can bring a staff viewpoint and perspective to discussion and debate; they act according to their own conscience. The school deals with balancing being both a member of staff and a governor by demanding behaviour which is, in effect, ethical, i.e. characterised by honesty and integrity, e.g.:

- never pressing a personal agenda
- being clear about what information can be reported back to colleagues
- being wary of bringing an individual issue or grievance to meetings without following agreed procedures
- keeping yourself aware of staff viewpoints and
- playing an active part in governor meetings and sharing in the wider governor workload.

Action

If you are considering promotion, reflect also on what you might learn from being a governor, in your own school or in another school. Have a look at (or construct) your own curriculum vitae (CV); examine what

> is missing. How could a spell as a school governor assist you in strengthening your claims to good knowledge of issues like strategy and finance? Don't just contemplate – act! It will improve your understanding of whole-school issues and leadership – and expand your ethical awareness.

This chapter about school governance has been brief because it is not a central concern for most classroom teachers or even for middle managers. However, as we have seen, to complete the circle of ethical procedures in school it is important that the governors are as knowledgeable in this area as the SLT, the middle managers and other school staff and students. There is a continuing professional development opportunity here for teachers by involving themselves with governance in their own or another school.

TEMPLATE FOR AN ETHICAL SCHOOL

I want to deal with two questions at the end of this chapter which emerge from both the chapter itself and the book as a whole; they are as follows:

- What should an ethically aware school look like in practice?
- How can a school be monitored for ethical awareness?

I am going to answer both of these questions at once. My suggestion is that, alongside other self-evaluation activities, schools should contemplate an ethical audit of their practice, and put in hand a small group of people to carry this out. Notionally, such an audit group might do this once or, at most, twice a year. The sections on how to improve performance in this area would have special significance; reflective learning is important. The audit document (Table 10.1) gives an indication of the kind of ground that would need to be covered. It could be easily adapted or extended to meet individual circumstances. It is not as onerous as it looks at first sight, because much of this information should already be available in other school monitoring contexts.

Table 10.1 Audit document: Aspects of an ethical school

Criteria	Typical evidence of good practice	Examples of less effective operation Any queries, failures, formal or informal complaints. What happened? Why? How? Lessons learned. How to improve?
Evidence of the school espousing key ethical principles:	Clear exposition of school's vision and mission Clear ethical statements in school policy documents	
Integrity – an open, fair and consistent approach to educational issues and management problems	SLT keeps staff in the loop about changes, consulting where possible	
Honesty – at all levels and for all employees	Open explanations and reasons for decisions	
Impartiality – a scrupulous approach to equality at all times with respect to both staff and students	Confidentiality preserved; opportunities open to all	
Respect – for everyone in the class and the school, or who visits the school	Manners and modes of address consistently positive	
Patience – avoiding irritation when students find things hard	Acceptance that failure of understanding may be a failure of explanation	
Concern – which includes knowing students well, and moulding one's own behaviour	Knowing everyone by name; being aware of any specific health or similar issues	

Table 10.1 (Continued)

Criteria	Typical evidence of good practice	Examples of less effective operation — Any queries, failures, formal or informal complaints. What happened? Why? How? Lessons learned. How to improve?
Propriety – students role-model on staff and are conscious of ethical problems and how to approach them	Student/staff involvement in community service and charitable activities	
Ethical professionalism		
Staff behave fully in line with their professional codes of conduct	Staff should show awareness of their statutory obligations and duties	
Ethical behaviour between staff members – staff always behave professionally, respectfully and honestly towards one another regardless of role or rank	This criterion should apply in both public and private situations: e.g. classrooms, corridors, staff rooms, offices – and in relation to school members and outsiders	
All staff have a sound track record of in-house Continuing Professional Development (CPD), and external subject and pedagogical updating as appropriate	Staff attendances at training and their involvement in, e.g., relevant learned societies or subject organisations should be celebrated, along with other activities such as consultancy	

(Continued)

142 ETHICAL GOVERNANCE

Table 10.1 (Continued)

Criteria	Typical evidence of good practice	Examples of less effective operation — Any queries, failures, formal or informal complaints. What happened? Why? How? Lessons learned. How to improve?
Ethical conduct in the content and delivery of lessons:		
Ethical conduct towards students – in the management of the class and in the standards of classroom behaviour	Review of incidents of excellent and poor behaviour in class and how these are handled	
	Appropriate publication of sanctions' policy	
Ethical conduct relating to learning practices and teacher performance – lessons are based on a sound curriculum which allows for debate, discussion and higher order thinking skills.	Live, ongoing and pertinent curriculum debate throughout the school Awareness of curriculum weaknesses, strategies to counteract these	
Lessons are • consistently well-prepared, • enthusiastic, interesting, • varied in teaching methods, • delivered without bias, using unbiased or balanced sources.	This list of lesson attributes should be monitored by the SLT and middle managers in department areas, on a formal basis, to ensure teachers are sustaining high standards of pedagogy	

Table 10.1 (Continued)

		Examples of less effective operation
Criteria	*Typical evidence of good practice*	*Any queries, failures, formal or informal complaints. What happened? Why? How? Lessons learned. How to improve?*
Student performance should be monitored using the techniques of • pertinent and immediate feedback, • careful marking and comments, • formal assessment as required.	Monitored as part of lesson observations and lesson plans by senior and middle management staff – visible in records kept	
<u>Ethical approaches to external agencies and the outside world</u>		
Provision is made to take care of all visitors to the school so that they feel welcome and valued	Procedures in place within the context of security for students	
Ethical conduct to parents and the whole school community –	This has whole school and individual teacher dimensions (where teachers deal directly with parents)	
the role of parents is respected, correct and timely information is given and flexible opportunities are available for discussion with teachers;	Formal information such as newsletters or electronic communication Formal opportunities, and those on request	
Governors are given appropriate access and involved in school activities where practicable	Governors should have welcome access, but criteria clear about their role	

(Continued)

Table 10.1 (Continued)

Criteria	Typical evidence of good practice	Examples of less effective operation — Any queries, failures, formal or informal complaints. What happened? Why? How? Lessons learned. How to improve?
All members of the school community adopt positive standards of support for one another and for the school as a whole	Involvement in extracurricular activity; willingness to represent the school in public fora	
All members of the school community go out of their way to promote a positive image of the school, of the teaching profession, and the importance of education	Might cover a range of behaviour from dress codes to involvement in community activities, committees etc as a school representative. Press mentions of the school, staff members or students	
Confidentiality and privacy	Requirements of General Data Protection Regulation (GDPR) carried out with respect to students' privacy regarding oral, paper and electronic data	
Use of e-learning	Students and teachers behave appropriately online; rules regarding plagiarism are kept	
Awareness-raising of ethical issues with students	Monitoring of how this affects curriculum content, assemblies and extra-curricular opportunities to explore ethical issues with students	

Note: This document can be adjusted to suit local circumstances

11

THE ONLY WAY IS ETHICS

HOW DO TEACHERS AND STUDENTS ACQUIRE ETHICAL AWARENESS?

The novel by John Mortimer [47], *Quite Honestly*, begins with the heroine claiming her ambition was merely to do some good in the world. Her boyfriend found this amusing and used to introduce her to acquaintances as a do-gooder. She ponders whether he would prefer a 'do-badder'. The book is a humorous account of the tensions between, good, bad, honesty, criminality and the underlying social mores which produce these in Society at large.

In the same way, this book began, in Chapter 1, by trying to establish definitions; by Chapter 2 it had moved on to one of its central assertions – that the focus of ethical behaviour in schools is to provide the very best for students. The other central tenet of this text is: students stand at the heart of effective schools, and the ethics which drive the school system. As the book has progressed, these statements have been viewed through multiple lenses. Through this process we have come to an appreciation that two key aims of the ethical school are to encourage ethical students, and students to be ethical. So, in this last chapter, we return to that theme.

How do the youngsters in our care acquire ethical behaviour? Of course, as teachers we talk about ethical dilemmas, we debate with our classes ethical decisions and courses of action in school and in the wider world, and we articulate ethical reasoning which emerges from the topics we study. But it is probable that none of these things is as important or persuasive as living ethics because the ethical approach rubs off on us all – teachers and students. We said it before: teachers are role models.

These last are massively difficult things to demonstrate and prove beyond doubt: they are visible, yet they defy hard evidence. It is a parallel problem to another which has always intrigued me: why do some people have a religious faith? Both phenomena require people to adopt a principled and life-changing stance towards something that is not tangible. Some years ago, I set out on a quest to try to get nearer to the answer to this question of faith. I wanted to explore the issue by interviewing people who had, or had lost, religious faith; but I came to the conclusion that this would have been too intrusive. Instead, I took the autobiographies of people who claimed to have a religious faith and explored in their writing the path they had travelled. Each was different, yet I decided that an influential factor was simply 'exposure'. Typical of this genre was Alan Titchmarsh [48], the gardening guru and media presenter. I have always been a fan of Alan. I know nothing about gardens or gardening, but I saw him as an instinctive teacher and that drew me to watch his programmes. Titchmarsh is known for horticulture but also as an interviewer, presenter (including *Songs of Praise*), and novelist. From modest origins, he became a respected plantsman: he could be considered to span arts and science. So let me consider his autobiographical journey at some length. His autobiography contains a confession of faith, which he calls a journey; while an intermittent church-attender, he retains an underlying belief.

The faith is unequivocal yet not born out of revelation but out of a lot of time spent in church as a choir boy – at services and choir practice. He calls it 'instinctive'. The habit stuck: his years in a cassock conditioned him to attend churches often, albeit irregularly. His use of churches is not always for services but for the atmosphere, and this seems to be a frequent view when people discuss faith. He identifies an emotional response: to music, to the fact that many churches seem to inspire a peace born of an unbroken chain of worship. He rejects evangelical heartiness, shudders at the exchange of *The Peace* with strangers, but enjoys the language of the Prayer Book, drawing his own conclusion that his very familiarity with it is significant.

Almost as an afterthought he adds a telling explanation. The punctuation in his text seems especially precise, as if he is struggling to articulate ideas from somewhere deep in the sub-conscious. To summarise: for him, faith is not accepting every word of Scripture but a conviction that goodness, love and thoughtfulness have a part to play in life.

In this case it is clear what faith is not. It is not revelatory, nor is it born primarily of rationality. Though close to his parents, his father's death did not result in abandonment of faith. He doesn't express any feeling that others should follow his lead to become believers. Indeed, he concludes articulating one's beliefs does not make faith deeper or more real.

There is habituation, connected to church attendance: the comforting and secure habits of youth die hard or not at all; he wanders away, gravitates back. The phrases 'instinctive' and 'natural' seem more about the rhythm of daily life than about a scientific explanation. Some of the pull that faith exerts comes from a degree of dependency. That dependency is based on the love of words and music; and also on the intangibles of consecrated places which tend towards the numinous. But in the end, none of this will do as an explanation. His postscript is the plainest statement one could ask for, of projectionism: the best in human life must have a basis in some Absolute reflected in a good (i.e. ethical) life.

If I am right about habituation, then I suspect that both faith and ethical consciousness can be acquired in the same ways. The frustration is that the path is a very tricky one to discern. I have a former student and friend who is equally interested to find this path. He is head of a school in Malta, he believes strongly that his school is ethically based, and he would love to know in more detail how to communicate this 'ethicality' to the students — to do so more effectively. So in his doctoral studies he is looking for that path, to make plain the elusive. Fr Mark Ellul [49] and I are on the same journey, but we begin from different places: he from the centre point of faith, me from non-faith. Our curiosity is identical. I am going to let Mark (with his permission) tell some of his journey in his own words (it is only a small part of his work, episodic and heavily edited — but I think it captures the flavour):

> Schools should help the student to reflect critically on their surroundings and help them come up with a conclusion of how to relate to the social structures and ideologies presented to them. Finding one's belonging in Society provides inner peace that leads to happiness. One can observe that throughout the ages

humanity has struggled to obtain this inner peace [50], which, according to Christian (and Jewish) tradition, was lost by the introduction of sin.

Humankind has used three main routes to try to achieve this inner peace. In ancient Greece, Aristotle had proposed the way of the median between two main extremes (vices): the virtuous route. During the 18th Century, Immanuel Kant propounded an approach of obeying principles that are absolute, principles that also try to safeguard the dignity of others. During the 19th Century, yet another route was proposed – the utilitarian route. While all three routes have their pros and cons, Christian tradition, influenced by the work of St Thomas Aquinas, Christianised Aristotelian thought.

Christian philosophy is substantially based on the virtuous outlook initially proposed by Aristotle and helps the student to understand him/herself, as an individual created by God, and in relation to Society. Individuals should be led to think of consequences beyond themselves, their personal desires and aspirations, to become a self-gift for others who are on the same pilgrimage. Much of this can doubtless be paralleled in other faiths than Christianity.

Building a virtuous individual is the result of interaction with the whole Society. Governments and political structures direct ideologies. These thoughts, in turn, shape the culture of a country and direct its wealth provisions. These provisions dictate and shape family ties and friendships while forming one's outlook of dealing with Society.

The family can be regarded as the first hub where individuals encounter a value system. Values dear to the family, shape the initial reality of the individual. Social media, in turn, influence the lives of individuals and one of the dangers is that the media often suggest how possessions should be used to achieve happiness. Media, thus, provide their own 'curriculum' that offers a particular interpretation of how one relates to reality.

As children grow, they form part of various groups; in turn, each of these groups provides a structure of acceptance based on norms dictated by the group. Through the social dynamics within the group, individuals would once again be provided with another 'curriculum' that shapes how they might interpret reality.

Nurseries and schools are the first institutions which are set to educate the next generation formally. Within these institutions, students encounter the first group of peers that are not chosen by preference and offer a testing ground for one's beliefs at the same level field. Through the daily interactions happening within these institutions, pupils learn how to relate to different social interactions. While helping the students to discover skills that are latent, adults at school guide pupils in integrating acceptable norms in doing so, they reinforce values and virtues.

Kidder [51] advocates that pupils should be exposed to core values, learn to identify them and be allowed to experience and exercise these values. Schools and similar institutions thus become agencies where one tests one's value structure, amends it and integrates a value hierarchy. This learning might not be intentional; however, through mimicking and abiding with what is accepted by the norm students start to form a specific values structure. The acquisition of basic moral principles is the basis of character education and becomes even more important in a multicultural context.

Everything that happens in school affects character education. Character education is a systematic approach that helps students improve their moral judgment and thinking. It instils fundamental values such as courage, loyalty, respect for others and self, honesty, responsibility, kindness; these form the basis of every healthy relationship. All activity, including the following of policies, affects the teaching of the curriculum and the instruction process. Thus, all activity within the school and school-related has a role in character education.

Schools are the communities that can allow for character development to happen; the social interactions that happen at school mimic Society. As with other tasks at school, learning-by-doing provides a sound backdrop to assimilate the material with which one is presented. This approach also holds for the integration of values; instruction should present complex tasks where students would have to engage in higher-order thinking. These tasks help individuals to move beyond their concept of self and integrate the ideas; in the process, they should be helped to become more sensitive and understand the needs of others within the community. This approach increases the socio-emotional capacity of individuals.

Schools thus become the institutions that offer a safe environment where students can reflect critically on how their actions are affecting others. If offered the right conditions at school, students might be helped to reflect on what they learn on a didactic level and extend it to the moral level by understanding how their knowledge might affect others. Teachers play a crucial influence on character formation.

Places of belonging, and the feeling of safety, are the primordial needs of every individual. By offering a safe environment where one feels supported to flourish, teachers will be riding on innate psychological needs and igniting the natural learning disposition of children. They should direct these dispositions to facilitate the integration of knowledge and application to the student's specific needs. Taking this student-centred approach motivates the students to learn. Feeling safe further motivates the students to engage in a critical analysis of their surroundings. The schools that take this approach provide a suitable platform where holistic education can take place.

'Holistic pedagogy concerns the development of the whole student and acknowledges the cognitive, social, moral, emotional and spiritual dimensions of education' [52]. This form of pedagogy goes beyond the prescribed curriculum as dictated by syllabi. Nor is it limited to the confines of the classroom. It happens when teachers interlink lessons with daily life experiences. Curricular material can thus be utilised to present moral dilemmas to the students. Intentionally providing limited resources for work can trigger teamwork and sharing, specific class placement can trigger mutual support. Reflective teaching helps one to integrate values within one's pedagogy.

Teachers that adopt this holistic pedagogical style teach for life and not for the exam. They instil in pupils the sense of responsibility that learning is a tool that helps them be sensitive to their surroundings. This sensitivity opens students to become more aware of self and more empathetic to the needs of others. It creates a safe environment where pupils could bond. Thus, schools foster for a primordial need of human beings; they create places of belonging where students can bloom.

St Augustine suggested that our hearts are restless until they find rest in the Lord; helping the individual to integrate this sense of self-gift and sensitivity towards others would help pupils arrive at the integration of this inner peace that is a gift of God.

ETHICAL APPROACHES AND EDUCATION: SOME OVERLAPS AND AGREEMENTS

I find Mark's words reassuring because he echoes, albeit from an alternative perspective, so many of the themes of this book about the routes to ethical conduct and the nature of ethical thinking. Let me just dwell on a few:

- Though I have tended to talk about pursuing 'the good' and he talks of achieving happiness or peace, i.e. through good actions, his notion clearly flows from mine
- We both emphasise the need to reflect on how our actions impact on others
- We both have reservations about social media as purveyors of values beyond the superficial
- We share a view of schools as miniature Societies
- We share a view of schools as value agencies
- Teachers as role models is a theme common to both
- We both promulgate the taught and hidden curricula of schools as vehicles of ethical learning and experience
- To this end we see schools as safe and inclusive environments with which ethical learning can take place
- We both emphasise the importance of reflective teaching which evaluates the ethical impact of pedagogy on students.

Mark's words sum up the arguments you have found in this text about ethical schools and ethical teaching. I do not share his roots in a theological system, but we are each searching for the same end as far as behaviour and attitudes are concerned, and importance of schools as the foundations of these. His next step in research is to demonstrate beyond doubt that these pathways of learning can be traced, that this holistic educative approach to developing character and ethical awareness works, and that students are able to be conscious of it and develop it themselves through self-knowledge. No mean task.

CLIMBING THE ETHICAL MOUNTAIN

Acquiring an ethical sense may be a long and uphill journey, over the ALPS if you like; but it is one worth making whether as a teacher or student. These are the aspirations of this book:

*Ethical **A**wareness*
*Ethical **L**iteracy*
*Ethical **P**ractice*
*Ethical **S**ufficiency*

FINIS

This book has demonstrated that teachers and the business of teaching exist in a world of ethical dilemmas. Effective teachers need:

- To articulate and live by an ethical philosophy of education and professionalism
- To plan and deliver curriculum which is ethical in intent and content
- To prepare and teach lessons which are driven by ethical approaches to pedagogy
- To encourage students to think about, learn and understand the ethical dimensions of their studies
- To forge a personal career around ethical principles
- To manage others in an ethical manner
- To become part of, and support, the ethical standards adopted by the school
- To help students develop into ethical beings, aware of the nature of ethical matters and ready to make ethical decisions themselves throughout their lives.

If one wanted to be poetic one might say that teachers swim daily in a sea of ethical dilemmas, whether they are helping students to learn, acting within the constraints of Society and of the school's management, or themselves acting as managers of colleagues. It is a never-ending process; one that cannot be ignored, evaded or avoided. The tides of ethics and education flow, hand in hand, through the portals of schools and the activities of teachers.

There is another dimension, too – one not touched on specifically in this book; but for completeness it needs to be mentioned. A hundred years ago, the doctor, the parson and the teacher in any community, would have been the repository of ethical standards and behaviour in their social setting. That era has gone. Yet there is a lingering suspicion that ethics cannot be turned off at the school gates. The question marks are: are teachers still seen as the upholders of ethical standards in the community? Should they be?

Taking ethical issues seriously is never easy. This has been a book about learning, and about the role which the teaching profession, classroom teachers and middle leaders specifically, play in delivering learning ethically and equitably. There are hundreds of thousands of children up and down the country who enjoy school, have supportive home environments, who flourish in school and out of it, flourish in academia, and are provided with the means to make a good life for themselves as stable, interested, and fulfilled adults. But there are others, too; the ones who have no support beyond school, who rebel against society all too readily, who are only too eager to believe that nobody cares (too often they don't). For them, teachers are a last hope. We are members of a proud profession, and one which is motivated not by self-interest but ethically, and overtly in the interests of others for the greater good. In the enduring spirit of the book, I am not going to finish with a high-flown academic quotation but with an allusion to a song. Mercifully (for you) I am not going to sing it. Dolly Parton, the Country and Western singer, in *The Seeker*, looks back on her own bleak childhood and reminds us that our charges have aspirations, but they may appear hopelessly unattainable. She has made caring for these disadvantaged children a part of her work for several decades, setting up a charitable foundation to support underprivileged students. For that small, but critically important, group of children, there is often only one hope: teachers. Ethics demand that every child matters.

NOTES AND REFERENCES

FOREWORD

The opening reference to the views of Gardner is from the title of an article by Gardner John W. and Rose, Pat (2009) *Journal of Advertising Education* from Sage Publications and accessible as http://doi.org/10.1177/109804820901300203.

CHAPTER 1

No notes.

CHAPTER 2

You can look up the current Code of Conduct for Teachers in England (Google: Department for Education: Teachers' Standards); there are plenty of other examples on the internet if you look around. See: https://www.gov.uk/government/publications/teachers-standards.

CHAPTER 3

1 The Scottish document is *Developing a Positive Whole School Ethos and Culture* – relationships, learning and behaviour published 21.06.18 and available on www.gov.scot website.
2 The BBC report was part of a series about this incident on 5th and 6th April 2020.
3 Ofsted produced a report about low level disruption and its detrimental effects on students' education: *Below the Radar: low-level disruption in the country's classrooms* (Department for Education 2014). This is available on the web at: https://www.gov.uk/government/publications/below-the-radar-low-level-disruption-in-the-countrys-schools.

4 FitzGerald, Penelope (1982) *At Freddie's*. London: Collins.
5 Ginott, H.G. (1972) *Teacher and Child: A Book for Parents and Teachers*. An updated version is published by New York: Three Rivers Press.
6 Andrew Marvell (1621–1676) wrote the poem *To His Coy Mistress* which used the ironic description of the grave as 'a fine and private place'. The poem can be found at https://www.poetryfoundation.org/poems/44688/to-his-coy-mistress.
7 Orly Shapra-Lishchinsky (2011) "Teachers' Critical Incidents: Ethical Dilemmas in Teaching Practice." *Teaching and Teacher Education*, 27: 648–656.
8 Dewey, John (1907) "The School and Social Progress." Chapter 1 in *The School and Society*. Chicago: University of Chicago Press, pp. 19–44.

CHAPTER 4

9 Andrew O'Hagan's (2006) allusion is from his tragic novel *Be Near Me*. London: Faber.
10 The allusion is to Mavis Cheek's (2000) *Mrs Fytton's Country Life* – an altogether more light-hearted text than O'Hagan's book (also from Faber).
11 Hyppolyte Taine compares the English unfavourably with the French in *Notes on England* published in instalments c. 1870.
12 Lawrence Stenhouse's work can be accessed by Googling Taylor & Francis Online site using the title Humanities Curriculum Project tag and following published and historical documents. It makes for interesting reading as some of the texts contain his pencilled notes.
13 *Curriculum for Excellence* is the Scottish National Curriculum and available via www.gov.scot/education-scotland/scottish-education-system/policy-for-scottish-education.
14 Learning and Work Institute (2017) *Healthy, Wealthy and Wise: the impact of adult learning across the UK* (accessible via website learningandwork.org.uk).
15 *Child Health and Education Study* can be found in 'Recent findings from the 1970 child health and education study' available in www.ncbi.nlm.nih.gov/pmc/article/PMC1438120. It describes the progress of the longitudinal cohort study based on all children born in England, Scotland and Wales in one week of April 1970.
16 Albrechtslund, A. (2007) "Ethics in Technology Design." *Ethics and Information Technology* 9: 68–72.
17 Annie Dillard is an American writer on wildlife themes. The account comes from her 1974 collection of nature writing *Pilgrim at Tinker Creek*.

CHAPTER 5

18 Bertrand Russell (1983) *The Collected Papers of Bertrand Russell Volume 29: Détente or Destruction*. London: Routledge.
19 Blishen, E. (1967) *The School that I'd Like*. London: Harmondsworth.
20 Davis, Lynn, Williams, Christopher, Yamashita, Hiromi (2005) *Inspiring Schools: A Literature Review – Taking up the challenge of pupil participation*. Carnegie Trust.
21 The Martha Boles (1992) quotes are from *Universal Patterns: The Golden Relationship – art, math and nature* ISBN-10: 0961450444.
22 Kerry, T (2015) *Cross-curricular teaching in the primary school*. London: Routledge.
23 Education Scotland has produced curriculum guidance as *Curriculum Guidance: building the curriculum 3 – a framework for learning and teaching* (2008).
24 Olusoga, D. "The history of British slave ownership has been buried: now its scale can be revealed" *Guardian* 12.07.15. Available on theguardian.com/world/2015/british-history-slavery-buried-scale-revealed.

CHAPTER 6

25 John Lubbock's quotation, though dated, is apt – it comes from The Pleasures of Life available on-line through Project Gutenberg.
26 Susan K. Green, Robert L. Johnson, Do-Hong Kim, Nakia S. Pope (2007) "Ethics in Classroom Assessment Practices: Issues and Attitudes." *Teaching and Teacher Education*, 23: 999–1011. Accessed via https://doi.org/10.1016/j.tate.2006.04.042.
27 Marzano, R. J. and Pickering D. J. (2007) "The Case for and Against Homework." *Educational Leadership*, 64.6: 74–79.
28 Kazmierzak, Karen (1994) "Current Wisdom on Homework and the Effectiveness of a Homework Checking System" available as ERIC Number: ED371868.
29 Kralovec, E. and Buell, J. (2000) *The End of Homework*. Boston: The Beacon Press.

CHAPTER 7

30 Carol Vorderman's maths scheme for young people can be found at https://www.themathsfactor.com/. It received massive acclaim from students and parents across many countries in 2020.

31 Martinus Hendrikus (Martijn) Benders (b. 23.07.71) is a Dutch poet and philosopher, and chief editor of literary magazine De Honingzaag. He deals in a number of educational issues through his academic interest in philosophy.
32 Glasgow's research is on-going but one source is: Parkes, A., Sweeting, H., Wight, D. & Henderson, M. (2013) "Do Television and Electronic Games Predict Children's Psychological Adjustment? Longitudinal Research Using the UK Millenium Cohort Study." *Disease in Childhood,* 98(5).
33 Jerman-Blažič, B and Klobučar, T. (2005). *Security and Privacy in Advanced Networking Technologies* NATO Science Series book 193. Amsterdam, Netherlands: IOS Press.

CHAPTER 8

34 Margaret J. (Meg) Wheatley has been a speaker, teacher, community worker, consultant, advisor, formal leader. She believes that leaders must learn how to evoke people's inherent generosity, creativity, and need for community.
35 The Unesco Report is available on http://www.iiep.unesco.org/en/our-expertise/teacher-careers
36 Henry Adams (1838–1918) was an American thinker and writer whose views were often controversial: but he struggled to apply big ideas. In 1910, Adams printed and distributed to university libraries and history professors 'A Letter to American Teachers of History'. In it, he proposed a theory of history based on the second law of thermodynamics and the principle of entropy: that all energy dissipates, order becomes disorder, and the earth will eventually become uninhabitable.

CHAPTER 9

37 The allusion to Mark Twain relates to DeVoto, Bernard (1940) *Mark Twain in Eruption: Hitherto Unpublished Pages about Men and Events.* New York: Harper & Brothers.
38 Mayur Ramgir is an expert on Java, and self-declared philanthropist whose work can be accessed at https://www.mayurramgir.com/.
39 John C. Maxwell is a pastor specialising in publishing texts about leadership. In 2014 he was named number one leadership and management expert in the world by *Inc.* magazine. *Inc.* is an American business magazine founded in 1979, in New York City, publishing eight print issues annually and daily online articles and videos.
40 J. R. R. Tolkien is universally known for his *Lord of the Rings* fantasy novel published in London by Allen and Unwin. The reference here is to one of his poems.

41 Colin Powell was a 4-star general who later became the first African American US Secretary of State; he is a great thinker about the art of leadership. You can read about his views on leadership in Harari, Oren (2002) *The Leadership Secrets of Colin Powell*. London: McGraw Hill ISBN: 0071388591.

CHAPTER 10

42 National Governance Association advice is available via their web-site at www.nga.org.uk.
43 The NAS/UWT course on staff governorship is currently (May 2020) advertised on https://www.nasuwt.org.uk/being-involved/training-and-development/training-courses/staff-governors.html.
44 The Schools Improvement article was posted on March 27 2013 and can be accessed at https://schoolsimprovement.net/staff-governors-do-we-need-them-should-we-have-them/.
45 Phil Revell's article in the Times Educational Supplement can be accessed at https://www.tes.com/i-would-be-a-teacher-governor.
46 Advice from City of York Council's Governor Support & Development Service (about teacher governance) can be obtained c/o Mill House, North Street, YORK YO1 6JD. Tel: 01904 554210.

CHAPTER 11

47 John Mortimer's (2005) satirical novel *Quite Honestly* from Viking (now Random House) is the source of this allusion – a book riddled with ethical question marks.
48 Alan Titchmarsh's autobiography *Trowel and Error* (2002) from Hodder & Stoughton is the source of this information.
49 Mark Ellul's work is quoted with his permission from a variety of papers supplied, which mostly relate to his Master's thesis for the University of Leicester MSc in Educational Leadership and his on-going PhD studies. Mark is a Roman Catholic clergyman in Malta, the head of a prestigious primary school, the Archbishop's Seminary School in Rabat. I have edited the order and (slightly) some wording to fit my text, but tried to remain true to his intentions.
50 Bullough Jr, R. V. and Pinnegar, S. (2009). "The Happiness of Teaching (as Eudaimonia): Disciplinary Knowledge and the Threat of Performativity." *Teachers and Teaching: Theory and Practice*, 15(2): 241–256.
51 Kidder, R. M. (2009). *How Good People Make Tough Choices: Resolving the Dilemmas of Ethical Living*. New York: HarperCollins (revised edition).
52 Tirri, K. (2011). "Holistic School Pedagogy and Values: Finnish Teachers' and Students' Perspectives." *International Journal of Educational Research*, 50: 159–165.

INDEX

ALPS 152
attitudes 43

Blishen, Edward 64, 66, 79, 157
Boles, Martha 73, 157

career options 118–120
Child Health and Education Study 54, 156
class management 24–41
classroom behaviour 33–35
Code of Conduct 14–16, 19–20
Code of Practice, school governance 133–134
Covid-19 44–45, 71, 99
curriculum, building 52–57
curriculum, content 44
curriculum, e-learning 102
curriculum, for health 53–54
curriculum, for wealth 56
curriculum, for wisdom 57
curriculum, formal 55
curriculum, inter-disciplinary 74–80
curriculum, philosophy of 47
curriculum subjects, English literature 50
curriculum subjects, geography 49, 59–60
curriculum subjects, history 49, 59, 76–79
curriculum subjects, literacy 58
curriculum subjects, mathematics 57–58
curriculum subjects, media and IT 60
curriculum subjects, personal and social 61
curriculum subjects, religion 50, 58
curriculum subjects, science 51, 58
curriculum subjects, technologies 61
curriculum subjects, visual arts 60

Dewey, John 41, 156

education, philosophy of 79
ethical assessment 86–90
ethical career paths 111–120
ethical class management 37, 70
ethical consciousness 27, 128–131, 145–152
ethical curriculum 42–63, 66, 83
ethical dilemmas viii, ix, 6–9, 20–23, 39–41, 80, 100, 153
ethical governance of schools 133–144
ethical guidelines 29
ethical issues, deconstruction of 7
ethical job seeking 112–115
ethical leaders, skills of 125–126
ethical lesson planning 83–85, 95–97
ethical literacy 19
ethical middle leadership 121–132
ethical pedagogy 64–81, 83
ethical principles 51–52
ethical school 139
ethical school audit 140–144
ethical teaching methods 65–67, 79
ethical terminology 3, 12

INDEX

ethics, and e-learning 98–110
ethics, and ethos 27–30, 33, 35
ethics, and everyday life 1–3
ethics, and faith 146–151
ethics, and sanctions 30–33
examinations and testing 71, 86

feedback 86–89
FitzGerald, Penelope 36, 156
Framework for Ethical Leadership in Education 129

Gardner, John William x
Ginott, Haim 36, 156
governor, staff 136–139
governors, chair of 133, 135
groups 5

headteacher 18, 31, 134–135
heutagogy 73
hidden curriculum 62
homework, ethical analysis 90–94

interdisciplinary learning 73–79

knowledge 43

law 18
leadership, courage in 131–132
learned societies 16
Learning and Work Institute 53, 156
learning, higher order 102
learning, interdisciplinary 103–104
learning, issues 101
lesson intentions 84, 93

marking 86–89
metacognition 70, 80
middle leaders vii, 44, 73, 85, 121–132, 154
morals 3

National Curriculum 44, 48
National Governance Association 134
norms 4

Ofqual 71
Ofsted 33–34, 44
Olusoga, David 77–79, 157

pedagogy 44, 47
pedagogy, holistic 150
principal 10, 21, 26
professionalism 11, 13–23, 106, 117

research 92
Russell, Bertrand 64–65, 157

self-analysis 111–112, 122–124
Senior Leadership Team vii, 26, 28, 35, 40, 82, 139
social media 9–10, 108, 148
social policy 55–56
Society 5, 28, 127
Standard Attainment Tests 31–32
Stenhouse, Lawrence 45–52, 156
students 16, 25, 29–32, 37–38, 41, 44, 66–68, 72–73, 86, 106, 153

Teaching Regulation Agency 18
teacher trainees vii, 20
teacher unions 16, 19
teachers vii, 12, 15, 20, 22–23, 25, 27, 29, 32, 34–36, 38, 45, 67, 72, 81, 86, 99, 106, 145, 153–154
teachers, as learners 68
teaching skill, of differentiation 69–70
teaching skill, of explaining 69, 82
teaching skill, of questioning 68

values 4, 43

whole curriculum 42

For Product Safety Concerns and Information please contact our EU representative GPSR@taylorandfrancis.com
Taylor & Francis Verlag GmbH, Kaufingerstraße 24, 80331 München, Germany

www.ingramcontent.com/pod-product-compliance
Lightning Source LLC
Chambersburg PA
CBHW071821230426
43670CB00013B/2522